Edmund S. Ffoulkes

The Church's Creed or the Crown's Creed?

a letter to the most Rev. Archbishop Manning, etc. Fifth Edition

Edmund S. Ffoulkes

The Church's Creed or the Crown's Creed?
a letter to the most Rev. Archbishop Manning, etc. Fifth Edition

ISBN/EAN: 9783337272968

Printed in Europe, USA, Canada, Australia, Japan

Cover: Foto ©Andreas Hilbeck / pixelio.de

More available books at **www.hansebooks.com**

The Church's Creed or the Crown's Creed?

A LETTER

TO

THE MOST REV. ARCHBISHOP MANNING,

ETC., ETC.

BY

EDMUND S. FFOULKES, B.D.,

AUTHOR OF "CHRISTENDOM'S DIVISIONS."

" First cast out the beam out of thine own eye, and then shalt thou see clearly to cast out the mote out of thy brother's eye."—*S. Matt.* vii. 5.

FIFTH EDITION.

LONDON:

J. T. HAYES, LYALL PLACE, EATON SQUARE.
NEW YORK:—POTT & AMERY.

N.B.—A few verbal corrections occur in this edition, that should have been made previously: and in two or three places about as many words, enclosed in brackets, have been added, to make the sense plainer.

London: Swift & Co., Regent Press, 55, King Street, Regent Street, W.

A LETTER,

&c.

My Lord Archbishop,

I take the liberty of putting the question to you in your official capacity, which forms the heading of my letter, and I invite public opinion in this country to weigh dispassionately whatever answer you may be pleased to return to it, or else to draw such conclusions from your silence as the nature of the case may suggest, should you resolve on letting it pass unheeded.

It is not, however, solely by any means on account of the exalted position which you occupy that I address myself to you. We were neither of us born or bred in the Communion in which we now are. The evidences which determined you to embrace the Communion of the Church of Rome, for the most part determined me likewise. You preceded and I followed: yet I neither followed you nor any one else blindly, as a party leader. According to the best of my judgment, I followed truth whithersoever it led me, and by whomsoever it was suggested. Still, I should be the last to deny—why should I not be always proud to acknowledge ?—the many difficulties that I had unravelled for me in my searchings after truth continually by yourself, by the inimitable lucidity and high-souled earnestness of your discourses as a preacher: and by the noble example of devotion and self-sacrifice which you exhibited as a servant of Christ, in acting to the uttermost up to what you believed to be true. The result of it all was that ultimately my convictions led me to follow in

B

your wake; though there are still others, whose profound learning, and honesty, and piety, I have never for one moment ceased to respect equally with your own, as deliberately convinced as ever of the righteousness of the position abandoned by us as untenable so many years ago. I was far from undervaluing their testimony, even when I subscribed to your own in preference: and once removed to our new abode, I must confess my course to have been deliberately the exact opposite to what I believe yours to have been ever since. You, and very many more probably, seemed to have joined the Roman Communion not only pledged never to find fault with it, but to see with its eyes, hear with its ears, understand with its understanding, stand or fall by its judgment. Your argument, I presume, would be that the Church of Rome claims to be infallible : that you submitted yourselves to it as such, in the fullest confidence that its decisions can never mis-lead you : that they are God's voice speaking to you, which you are bound at the peril of your salvation never to mistrust, much less dispute. I joined the Roman Communion on other grounds, and was accepted. Practically, no doubt, the Church of Rome claims to be infallible, and anybody who concedes, is dearer to her than anybody who disputes, her claim : but I was never required to profess this on entering her Communion, and perhaps might never have entered it, if I had been. " Sanctam catholi-cam et apostolicam Romanam Ecclesiam, omnium ecclesiarum matrem et magistram, agnosco," a medieval phrase, of which I knew the full historical value, was the uttermost to which I gave my adhesion. And I said to myself on that occasion, if she is really infallible, she can stand much more searching criticism than the one which I am leaving for her sake, on behalf of which no such claim has ever been made. For I considered that after the extreme rigour with which the claims of the Church of England had been examined by us all, it would be the height of disingenuousness in us to shut our eyes to any weak points of the system that we were embracing in preference, should any such exist. I felt that if I found the claims of the Church of

Rome to be thoroughly in accordance with facts, I should ever afterwards regard her with tenfold reverence from having verified them myself. If they were true, analysis, impartially conducted, could only confirm them : if they were false to any extent, or exaggerated, I conceived we should be bound in common honesty to tell our friends that we were to that extent, in reality, no better off than we had been where we were before. But till I had actually been received into communion with Rome, it was my own impression, and I was assured by members of the Roman Communion over and over again, that I could never judge of her system at all fairly or adequately : and this was one of my chief reasons for embracing it when I did. Afterwards I resided in various countries where it was dominant, and studied its worship in town and country, comparing them with what I had abandoned for it at home. Then I returned and set myself to work to improve my previous knowledge of its history in past ages, and its relations with other Churches : paying especial attention to the causes which had produced estrangement between it and them for a time, or till now. All this has been my constant employment for the last dozen years or more : so that I cannot be said to have drawn my conclusions hastily. Now this occupation, and the temper of mind which is the fruit of it, whether you approve of it or not in those who have become members of the Church of Rome, you certainly seem to wish to encourage in those who are still members of the Church of England. You criticise their system, and invite their criticising it under your guidance. You appeal to them as men of fairness and honesty to listen to you, and to take to heart what you say. Should they find it to be true, then your advice to them is to abandon a Communion against which so many objections exist which they cannot answer, for another which you represent to them as infallible—I refer more particularly to your well-known, and most persons will admit, appositely-timed, letters on the Crown in Council—" The Crown in Council on the Essays and Reviews : " and "The Convocation and the Crown in Council." Whether you ever received any reply from the "Anglican friend" to whom they were addressed, I am unable to say: but I presume that when you wrote you must have contemplated the possibility of his rejoining, and that you were prepared to attend to any counter statement coming from him in the same spirit of candour and impartiality in which he had been invited to listen to you: that in the event of his succeeding to retort the difficulty with which you had pressed him, you would not have been above looking it full in the face, and endeavouring to explain it to his satisfaction: or else, if you felt obliged to admit that it could not be explained satisfactorily, you would never have condescended to have recourse to any subterfuge that you would have condemned in him, but would have confessed yourself answered. Allow me, therefore, for the time being, to personate your Anglican friend: conceive that it is he who speaks: imagine him accredited to speak in the name of all those whom you have addressed through him as well as his own, and to rejoin as follows—

"I might admit every word that has fallen from you on the power exercised amongst us of the Church of England by the Crown in Council, without being the least obliged to follow you to your deductions from it, for this simple reason, that 'two blacks don't make a white.' There has been, and is, too much of the 'Crown in Council' by half, if all that I hear is true, in your Communion as well as our own. In my humble opinion, we may fairly claim to have learnt our lesson from you, to have copied the example which you set us in our infancy, and to have faithfully followed out your own principles, according to the circumstances in which we were placed. I will not inquire whether, in virtue of the well-known Sicilian monarchy, the descendants of King Roger have not, or at least might not have, exercised the same authority 'in all causes, and over all persons, ecclesiastical as well as civil,' by favour of the Pope, that the descendants of Henry VIII. have ever succeeded in exercising, in spite of the Pope: but answer me this one question honestly. The creed which you and the

Archbishop of Canterbury recite still in common at each cele-
bration of the Lord's Supper, is it the Church's Creed or the
Crown's Creed? I will tell you the grounds which have convinced me irrevocably that it is the latter. I have read some-
where, and seen the original authorities cited at length in proof
of it, that this is its history. There were two forms of this
Creed rehearsed and authoritatively promulgated by the Fourth
Œcumenical Council: the Nicene, and the Constantinopolitan.
In neither of them, in the article relating to the Holy Ghost
and His procession, are those words found, ' and from the
Son.' The Council went on to say in its formal definition that
this Creed, as it had just been rehearsed, ' explicitly taught
(ἐκδιδάσκει), the perfect doctrine (τὸ τέλειον), concerning the
Father, Son, and Holy Ghost.' Besides asserting this dogmatically, ' the holy and Œcumenical Council'—I am quoting
the exact words in each case—' decreed that it was lawful for
nobody to propose, that is, compile, put together, hold, or
teach others, another faith. Those who dared either to put together another faith, or produce, teach, or deliver another symbol
to any desirous of returning to a knowledge of the truth from
Hellenism, Judaism, or any heresy whatsoever, were, if bishops
or clergy, to be deposed: if laymen, to be anathematised,' all
which was recited word for word, and re-affirmed with equal
solemnity—creed, canon, and definition alike,—by the Fifth and
Sixth Councils in succession. And could their meaning admit of
any doubt, it could be shewn by reference to every contemporary
writer or writing that deals with it, to amount to this: that not
a word was ever to be taken from or added to this Creed, as it
then stood, and, with the single deviation above-mentioned,
stands now. Most explicit on this head was the oath taken by
the Popes themselves. According to the earliest form preserved *
in their ' *Liber Diurnus*,' as it is called, every Pope on his elec-
tion swore to preserve unmutilated the Decrees of the first five
Councils, and, in a subsequent clause, of the sixth as well,

* Migne's Patrol., tom. cv. p. 40.

'*usque ad unum apicem*'—to teach all they taught, and to condemn all they condemned. By this, he was pledged *à fortiori* to their Creed, '*usque ad unum apicem,*' in the same degree. '*Si præter hæc aliquid agere præsumpsero, vel ut præsumatur permisero, eris mihi (Deus), in illâ terribili die judicii depropitius,*' was the imprecation which he was made to pronounce on his own head, in the event of his proving faithless to his obligations. I call especial attention to these words, because I find them cancelled in the Pontifical oath of the eleventh century; and by that time, though the innovation had received several checks in its progress, I find all the Churches of the West, with that of Rome at their head, using the Creed of which I have spoken, with those words added to it, 'and from the Son.' But I look in vain for any canon or definition of any General Council authorising or enjoining their insertion. I look in vain for any Papal Encyclic, such as that which emanated from the reigning Pope when the Immaculate Conception of the Blessed Virgin was made a dogma, proclaiming that they had been, or explaining why they had been, inserted with his full sanction. On the contrary, I find from authentic history, that they were first introduced into the Creed by stealth, and ultimately maintained there by force; the power striving for their introduction being pre-eminently that of the 'Crown in Council,' and the power resisting it that of the majority by far of the contemporary Church, backed by the Pope, to say nothing of all the previous Œcumenical Councils to which they appealed. You will correct me, if I am guilty of any historical mis-statement. I find, then, that its original introduction was due to a king, named Reccared, of a barbarous, and, till then, heretical race in Spain, who, A.D. 589, in the act of abjuring Arianism, promulgated the Creed in question ignorantly or wilfully, with this addition, at the head of the bishops of his dominions, many of them neophytes from Arianism like himself. No pope could have taken the lead more in the doctrinal as well as the disciplinary enactments of this Council, the third of Toledo, than the king did then. Nobody conversant with its acts can deny this. Such was what may therefore be called the lay-baptism of the new clause. So obscure was its origin, that it was not so much as noticed at the sixth Council, where the Creed was once more promulgated in the exact form settled by the fourth Council, as if nothing had happened. But in the eighth century, just before the seventh Council met, the Emperor Charlemagne—I say emperor by anticipation—happened to be on extremely bad terms with the Imperial Court of the East. More than this, the brother of the new Patriarch of Constantinople, S. Tarasius, who took the lead at the seventh Council, was a prisoner of war in his hands, having been captured in a hostile encounter with his forces in Italy. The Council, however, met A.D. 787, legislated, and was confirmed by the Pope, who forwarded its decrees, as well as his own approval of them, to Charlemagne. Charlemagne, fired with rancour against the East, immediately set about composing a work to refute them; and when it was ready for publication, summoned a Council at Frankfort of all the bishops of his dominions, at which the decrees of the seventh Council were formally repudiated, and his own work, which he, with the assistance of his theologians, had written against them, approved. This work he forwarded to the Pope, who had confirmed them. One of his principal charges against them was, that the Council enacting them had been silent or ambiguous on a point which he deemed it his duty to prove to the Pope at great length, namely, the Procession of the Holy Ghost from the Son: in other words, that while it had received a profession of faith from the new Patriarch, in which procession *through* the Son was affirmed, it had said nothing at all on that subject in its own Creed, with which he was therefore dissatisfied, as wanting the addition which had been made to it in Spain by King Reccared.

"What defence the Pope made for S. Tarasius we need not pause to inquire: but this is what he says in reply to the objection urged by the monarch against the Creed.

"'We have already proved the divine dogmas of this Council

irreprehensible, as the works of the principal of the holy Fathe abundantly testify. For should anybody say that he differs from the Creed of the above-named Council, he risks differing (or seems to differ), with the Creed of the six holy Councils : inasmuch as these Fathers spake not of themselves, but according to what had been holily defined and laid down before : as it is written in the book of the sixth holy Council, amongst other things, ' This Creed had been sufficient for the perfect knowledge and confirmation of religion . . . for concerning the Father, Son, and Holy Ghost, what it explicitly teaches is perfect.'

" I ask you, my Lord, as a plain-spoken Englishman, whether it would be possible to conceive the Creed of the Church more deliberately impugned by the Crown in Council in the teeth of the Pope ? I am persuaded at all events that there has been nothing approaching it in the history of the Church of England since the Reformation. Charlemagne, as the mouth-piece of the Council of Frankfort, composed of his own subjects or allies, took formal objection to the Creed of the Church, as it then stood, and had just been promulgated for the fourth time by a General Council confirmed by the Pope, because in the article defining the procession of the Holy Ghost it wanted those words ' and from the Son : ' and the formal answer of the Pope thus appealed to was, that its explicit teaching was perfect, though it wanted those words.

" Yet the 'Crown in Council,' we must conclude, was more intimately versed in theology than either the Church in Council or the Pope, for it carried its point after all—either this, or the Church of Rome in adopting those words submitted to its dictation : for there is no other alternative. Still, for some time matters remained as they were : Charlemagne seems to have taken no further action in public for the moment, though he went on using the addition of King Reccared in singing the Creed in his own chapel. Whether it was at his instigation or not that some monks of his empire carried it afterwards to Jerusalem, and deliberately made a parade of it in one of the Eastern

Patriarchates, where they had obtained a footing, is perhaps uncertain, though far from improbable. Two things are certain : 1, that the Easterns at once detected and unanimously condemned the innovation ; and 2, that the monks excused themselves, as far as the Creed was concerned, by pleading that it was so sung in the Imperial chapel. This had the effect of reviving the discussion, which the Emperor, if he had not contrived himself, lost no time in coming forward to settle in his own way. At the head of his bishops once more, he expounded what he considered to be the orthodox doctrine on the subject in question to the Pope, and this time it was a Pope greatly beholden to him— Leo III.—and ended by requesting to have his adopted version of the Creed authorized. This time the Pope admitted his doctrine to be correct, but would have nothing at all added to the Creed. ' As I understand, then,' rejoined one of the Imperial deputies, ' your Paternity orders that the clause in question be first ejected from the Creed, and then afterwards lawfully taught and learnt by anybody, whether by singing, or by oral tradition.' 'Doubtless that is my desire,' returned Leo : ' and I would persuade you by all means so to act.' That the Pope had great misgivings as to whether his instructions would be obeyed, is evidenced by his having the Creed subsequently engraved in Greek and Latin, *without those words*, ' and from the Son,' on two silver shields, and hung up in the most conspicuous place of his church, '*pro cautelá orthodoxæ fidei*,' as he said himself, and not merely that the Creed might remain intact. That his misgivings were well founded is proved from what Æneas, Bishop of Paris, reported about fifty years after : namely, that the whole Gallican Church chanted it every Sunday in the form for which Charlemagne had contended. Previously to this, its admirers, in endeavouring to import it into Bulgaria, had elicited a much more angry protest from the East than when it was first tried at Jerusalem. But, meanwhile, the party that had twice disobeyed Rome in retaining it, had made themselves so useful to Rome in other respects that they had disarmed her opposition.

Two centuries more, and Rome herself conformed to their Creed, silently and clandestinely : no decretal, encyclical, or synodical, announcing her adhesion. The thing was done in a corner, and but for a curious liturgical writer of the Western Empire, who went to see his sovereign Henry II. crowned at Rome, A.D. 1014, by the Pope, nobody could have guessed when it occurred. Berno therefore records what he witnessed with his own eyes and ears : and being engaged himself in a work on the Mass, he would naturally be very particular in his inquiries when he came to Rome, of all places, how things were done there. Now his account is that, 'up to that time the Romans,' that is, the Church of Rome generally, 'had *in no wise* chanted the Creed after the Gospel : but that the lord emperor Henry would not desist, till with approval of all he had persuaded the apostolic lord Benedict to let it be chanted at High Mass.' There has been a vast amount of learning expended on this passage, but the only Creed chanted at Mass in the West then being the interpolated Creed adopted by Charlemagne, it stands to reason that no other could have been pressed upon the Pope by the Emperor. Hence, whether or not it had been in use there previously, it was now for the first time ordered to be chanted at High Mass there after the Gospel, as it had long been elsewhere throughout the West, in deference to if not by command of the Emperor. Benedict had been restored from exile by Henry the year before, and therefore was pledged on every account to consult his wishes, yet it seems to have cost him a struggle to give way on this point.

"Thus Reccared inaugurated the addition : Charlemagne patronised it : and Henry II. got it adopted by the Popes themselves. When this had been done, the pontifical oath was changed. Later Popes of course shrank from imprecating a judgment upon themselves, according to the terms of their oath, in case they failed to keep the decrees of the General Councils enumerated in it, '*usque ad unum apicem*,' when they felt they had notoriously failed to do so by the Creed. That clause was accordingly struck out. In the corresponding clause of the oath that was afterwards taken by them—the way in which Cardinals are mentioned in it associates it with the well-known decree of Nicholas II., 1059, respecting the Sacred College—they are made to say simply, 'May God be merciful to me in that awful day if I do my diligence to keep all these things sworn to by me.' Had it been intended to intimate that they had been now and then forced to do otherwise, it could not have been differently worded.

"How, after this, the Creed used by us both in our Liturgy can be called the Church's Creed, and not the Crown's Creed, I am at a loss to comprehend : how Rome can, after this, be exculpated from the charge of having succumbed to the '*Crown in Council*,' infinitely more than England, I should be pleased in all honesty to learn from you. For this, as I presume you would admit, is no mere matter of 'antiquarian research' or 'dreary speculation.' The formal definitions of the Church are still as obligatory, still as dogmatically correct, as when first promulgated. And one of them, repeated by a series of General Councils in the same words, says that what the Creed taught explicitly with reference to the Trinity was perfect when it was without those words, 'and from the Son.' Now, to contend that there can be any further explanation of that which is explicitly perfect already, is to deprive words of their obvious meaning and to insult common-sense. The majority by far of the Church was with Adrian I. and Leo III. when they defended the uninterpolated Creed against Charlemagne : the majority by far of the Church was against Benedict VIII. when he yielded to the threats or persuasion of Henry II. The same majority of the Church broke off communion with the Pope for abandoning, and finally submitted to be annihilated and cut off from the face of the earth itself, sooner than abandon the Creed of the Church for that of the Crown. I am utterly unable to see where the parallel fails in principle. Reccared, Charlemagne, and Henry II., prescribed a Creed for the West, at least as much as Henry VIII.,

Edward VI., and Elizabeth, prescribed one for England. Subsequent acceptance cannot alter their origin in either case : and whether one consisted in a compound word of four syllables, and the other in thirty-nine articles, embodying six hundred propositions, the fruits were the same ; a schism in each case followed, and both schisms are still in force. When the West separated from the East, the East constituted the majority of the Church by far ; when England separated from Rome, the majority of the West by far sided with Rome. Thus it came to pass that Rome was literally paid back in her own coin. Adding to the Creed of the Church produced one schism : subtracting from the Creed of the Church of Rome another. The Reformation was at once the avenger and the logical offspring of the schism between the East and West. The West became a prey to disunion, split into fragments, and had its own Creed questioned, retributively for its conduct towards the East, which it trampled on for upholding the Creed of the Church. Then if Anglican orders are denied by Rome, Western orders may be confronted by Creed, Canon, and Definition of the fourth, fifth, and sixth Councils : by their definition affirming their creed to be perfect as it then stood: by their canon ordaining that any bishop or clergy substituting another creed for it as it then stood should be deposed. Unless this canon is to be construed in a non-natural sense, I cannot see that there is much to choose between Anglican and Roman orders : as to this day its operation must extend to every bishop and priest in the West using the Creed of Reccared and Charlemagne instead of that of the Church. If its operation has become obsolete, it is because the power of enforcing it has passed away : in other words, because the executive of the Church is defunct, negligent, or unable to act. Let me add a few words on the nature of the Canon. For some time past a misconception has been prevalent respecting this Canon which has impaired its force. People have spoken of it in general as the seventh Canon of the Council of Ephesus, and therefore regarded it as any other Canon of a General Council ; and with neither more nor less reverence. This account of it is far short of the truth. It was indeed first promulgated at Ephesus, but it was not intended to apply to any but the original form of the Nicene Creed then, that form alone having been used there, as we learn from the 'Acta.' And it came seventh in order of the Canons passed there. But it was re-enacted under very different circumstances at the Council of Chalcedon, where it appears no longer among the canons, but immediately follows the definition. The Nicene Creed in its original form, and the same Creed in the enlarged form given to it by the Council of Constantinople, having been both recited and authoritatively placed on the same footing by the Council, the formal definition of the Council was then appended to them, and to it this Canon. Thus a new rank was given to it, which the fifth and sixth Councils alike confirmed. It ceased to be a canon in the ordinary sense of the word, and became a dogmatic canon, of as permanent and universal obligation as the definition itself to which it was appended : just, for instance, as the judgment appended by the Nicene Fathers themselves to their Creed. ' Those who say there was a time when He was not,' and so forth. As well might the Popes have consented to any modification of these clauses as of this Canon.

"There is one more point in connection with it that I would fain submit for your more special consideration before I conclude, namely, what justification can you and your subordinates plead for your modern practice, so directly opposed to this Canon, of requiring all who come over to you from Anglicanism to recite and testify their acceptance of the Creed of Pope Pius, when this Canon, as binding as ever on the whole Church, ordains expressly, that persons coming over to the Communion of the Church, *from any heresy whatsoever*, shall have the Nicene Creed, and no other, proposed to them for their acceptance ? Every time you violate this injunction, you incur the penalty denounced against such by the Church that has lost her voice. This is surely something like living in a glass house yourself, my Lord—I beg you will excuse the metaphor—is it not ?"

Such, then, is the answer which I conceive Anglicans might fairly make to your letters on the "Crown in Council"—by publishing them you must have intended them for more than one—and I give publicity to it both on their account in order that they may adopt it if they think fit, and on my own, to satisfy the dictates of my conscience whether they adopt it or not. For I feel it imperative to state publicly to them and to you how materially my inquiries into this one question have modified my estimate of the Roman claims, and though the re-union of Christendom, which has been the dream as well as the prayer and study of my whole life, seems absolutely looming in the distance, I desire to record my solemn conviction, that it cannot be, that it ought not to be, till material guarantees have been secured that Rome shall never again be what she has been, and to some extent still is : so irresistible to my mind are the evidences that it is her conduct, more than anything else, which has divided Christendom—her conduct since she became a Court as well as a Church—not her faith, but her policy for the last thousand years, dating from her endowment under Charlemagne. Eminent saints and doctors of the middle ages, if they mean anything, have asserted as much : I have nothing to do but adopt their language : their denunciations were loudest when they were by no means levelled against the particular vices of this or that Pope. S. Bernard is not attacking his old pupil Eugenius, when he tells him in unvarnished language of the " murmurs and complaints of the Churches " of his day.* " They cry loudly that they are mutilated and dismembered. . . . Abbots are exempted from bishops, bishops from archbishops, archbishops from primates or patriarchs. Can this be good in theory : can it be excused in practice ? . . . Can you possibly think it lawful for you to dismember the Church, confound order, disturb the boundaries which your fathers have set ? If it be just for each to preserve his own rights, how can it accord with justice to take from a person what belongs to him ? You err, if you think that your Apostolic power, as it is

* De Consid. iii. 4.

the highest is the only power ordained by God. . . . Your power is by no means the only power from God: there are likewise intermediate and still lower powers—and as they are not to be separated whom God has joined, so neither are they to be made one whom He has divided?" "I remember once," says John of Salisbury, "going as far as Apulia, to see my lord Pope Adrian"—his countryman and ours, the English Pope—"who had admitted me to very great intimacy, and I passed nearly three months with him at Beneventum. In the course of conversation, of which we had at least the average amount that friends usually have, he asked me frankly and earnestly what men thought of him and of the Church of Rome. I told him in reply, very candidly and explicitly, the evil things which had come to my ears in the provinces. For, as was said by many, the Roman Church, which is the mother of all Churches, exhibits herself to the rest rather in the light of a step-mother, than of a mother. . . . . As for the Roman Pontiff, he is a universal oppressor, and well-nigh past endurance. . . . . That is what is said by the people, most holy Father, since you ask me to tell you what people say."*

"O Pope," exclaimed the great prophetess of the north by revelation, after three more centuries had passed: "thou art worse than Lucifer, more unjust than Pilate, more of a foe to me than Judas, more of an abomination to me than the Jews themselves."† Not that she was speaking of the vices of any one Pope in particular, but of the Papacy, such as it was then. I could fill pages from medieval writers of approved name to the same effect. What they meant, and what with history before us we cannot venture to contend they denounced extravagantly, were the principles and practices of a system known and stigmatised as the Court of Rome, for this was its head-quarters, which had clearly been inaugurated under Charlemagne and his successors, parties to the "donation," and had

---

* De Nugis Cur. vi. 23.
† Mansi, tom. xxx. pp. 715—18, with Cardinal Turrecremata's comments.

usurped precedence of the self-denying mould and pastoral gifts inherited from S. Peter. Their sway was no sooner established, than bad Popes found themselves omnipotent to do mischief, and the best Popes comparatively powerless to do good. Eugenius III. had not commenced, and he was impotent to resist, the changes in the constitution of the Church so bitterly denounced and deplored by S. Bernard.

All this I knew, and had well considered long before I joined the Roman Communion, as my books testify. I thought then, and am doubly convinced now, after reading ecclesiastical history through again as a Roman Catholic, that if ever there was a justifiable revolt from authority, it was the revolt we call the Reformation: and most certainly had it been a revolt from a mere secular power, like that of the United States of America from England, I for one should never have dreamt of transferring my allegiance from the Anglican to the Roman Communion, any more than I suppose any citizen of the United States in his sober senses would now dream of transferring his on principle to the British Crown. But all Scripture told me that there should be but one Church: and all history told me that a Primacy from time immemorial in that one Church belonged to the see of Rome: all history told me, moreover, that from the foundation of the see of Canterbury to the Reformation, the Church of England had been one with Rome, had voted freely and deliberately for the doctrine and discipline upheld by Rome, including the supremacy of the Pope, for centuries; and was at least as responsible for the corruptions that had accumulated in the middle ages and precipitated the catastrophe of the sixteenth century, as any other of the Churches in communion with Rome on the continent. Hence, it certainly seemed to me that the Church of England had done wrong in separating from the body of which she had been so long a foremost member, and affecting to care for nothing so long as her own boat got off safe, instead of standing manfully by her colours, and assisting by every means in her power to bring the old ship safe into port. At all events what excuse was there for our continued isolation ? If I could trust to the Roman Catholic divines of this country, whose teaching I took to be faithfully reflected in a work entitled the " Faith of Catholics," reprinted in 1846, for the third time, by a living dignitary, since promoted, and dedicated to the late Bishop Walsh, I felt there was nothing in the Roman Catholic system *now*, to which I could not honestly, and would not willingly subscribe, for the sake of breaking down the barriers that estranged us from the Churches abroad, with which our forefathers had lived and died in happy communion. It may be that I trusted those divines too implicitly : it is not long since I heard the term " minimisers" applied from the pulpit by a living preacher, who may be supposed your mouth-piece, to those who believed no more : though it would be difficult to produce any Roman Catholic catechism in use throughout England in which more was taught. But this by the way. More intimate acquaintance with the Continental Churches, and a much more searching investigation into the merits of the schism between the East and West than I had ever been able to give to it before, has modified my views on the whole question considerably between England and Rome. Let me begin with the last first.

To the facts, which some pages back I put into the mouth of your Anglican friend, you will doubtless remember my calling your attention privately just twelve months ago. Your only reply to me, so far as they were concerned, was that they were already known. This I construed as an admission on your part that I had stated them correctly. But if so, what other inference can be deduced from them, than that for the last 1,000 years the Roman Communion has been committed to the use of a Creed which is not that of the Church, but of the Crown ? I do not say *therefore* to the use of a Creed which is heterodox. On the theological question involved in it I would wish to speak with becoming reverence : but thus much is certain, that the addition which forms its distinguishing feature was made and had been in use many centuries before any Pope judged it allow-

c

able, much less necessary: many centuries before theologians in the West had agreed amongst themselves whether the terms "mission" and "procession" were distinguishable. Doubtless it has since found able defenders: but among them there are scarce two who give the same account of it, historically or doctrinally: and some of them are neither consistent with each other nor with themselves. Others, in arguing for it against the Easterns, have grievously mis-stated facts, and numberless passages have been adduced in support of it from the Fathers, either wholly spurious or interpolated. I know of no parallel to it in this respect in any religious controversy, before or since. If the Athanasian Creed was not expressly coined for this controversy, it was employed in this controversy first as a polemical weapon. At Florence, where the whole question of the Creed was gone into formally for the first time, the number of spurious passages adduced on the Latin side stands out in painful contrast to what was produced on the Greek side, in which even modern criticism has not been able to discover a single flaw. In the Florentine definition itself there is one clause which runs as follows : " We define that those explanatory words, ' and from the Son,' were to the end that the truth might be elucidated, under the necessity which existed then, lawfully and with good reason added to the Creed." The history of this clause is that it was urgently required by the Pope, who was present, and presided in person, as urgently resisted by the Easterns, and only conceded on the express understanding that it was not to prejudice their own use of the Creed in any way. What it means has yet to be shewn. Admit it historically, and it binds us to affirm that those words were " lawfully and with good reason added to the Creed " two centuries before Rome was so much as consulted on them : four centuries before she received them herself. Admit it dogmatically, and what follows? I take my stand on the definition of the fourth, fifth, and sixth Councils, and affirm the explicit teaching of the Creed on the Trinity perfect, as it stood then : namely, *without* those words, " and from the Son." This makes

me deny by implication all that this clause asserts: for how, I repeat, can *explicit* teaching which is *perfect*, admit of any further explanation? I must assert the contrary to this, or get over its obvious and genuine meaning in some shifty way, to be able to attach any dogmatical value to the Florentine clause: or else I must fall back upon the history of the Florentine clause once more. S. Antoninus, afterwards Archbishop of Florence, who was present at the Council, and a great canonist, says of those words, " and from the Son," emphatically: " It is certain, nor is it to be believed that they were added unless by some Pope or Council, for who else would have presumed to have added them? albeit by what Pope or Council is by no means certain." *
It seems hardly possible to doubt that the Florentine clause was framed on this hypothesis, and must be regarded accordingly, now that the facts are known. S. Antoninus, we may be sure, never contemplated our believing what we know to be not fact. The remainder of the definition, good and excellent as it is, in reality left the main point untouched. That is to say, it explained and harmonised the arguments by which the Greeks and Latins had defended their respective views *since the schism*, accommo-dated their views to each other, and ruled what should be taught in future by both: but it had not a word to say on what had been the doctrine of the Whole Church before the schism commenced: when Council after Council had declared the explicit teaching of the Creed on the Trinity to be perfect, as it stood then. To this Mark of Ephesus had called the attention of the Council in the most formal manner, by reciting their acts: but here pre-cisely the definition stopped short, as if by instinct or from design, and said nothing. So far from determining the relation which the two forms of the Creed, the old and the interpolated, bore to each other—to the amazement, as we are told, of the ambassadors from England who came to the Council—it neither recited nor alluded to any Creed at all, much less promulgated either form as the Creed of the Church. It abstained from

* Chron. P. III. tit. iii. c. 13, § 13.

c 2

affirming them identical : it abstained from pointing out how they differed : it gave no directions of any kind about their use. If the use of the old Creed was not interdicted for the future, neither was the use of the interpolated Creed enjoined. In conclusion, as if to stamp the whole business—as if to typify the union between the Creed of the Crown and the Creed of the Church that had taken place—both Emperor and Pope subscribed to the definition of faith side by side, a prodigy without parallel in the annals of Œcumenical Councils, before or since.

Therefore, my Lord, with the facts of this controversy before me, I find this conclusion inevitable : that whether absolutely inerrant or not in matters of faith herself, Rome has abundantly proved, during the last 1,000 years, that she can be a most negligent, hesitating, fickle, self-seeking, hypocritical guide to others, even where the Faith is concerned. Such, at all events, has been her conduct by the Church's Creed ; each epithet describes it at each stage : the last, the worst. Sad presage for the re-union of Christendom, in a General Council presided over by the Pope, that the only General Council [of the East and West] over which a Pope ever presided in person should have been the only Council ever convened exclusively for restoring union to the Church—I am using a phrase of the Pope who held it—and this the Council of Florence under Eugenius IV. ! Of all Councils that ever were held, I suppose there never was one in which hypocrisy, duplicity, and worldly motives, played a more conspicuous or disgraceful part. How the Council of Basle was outwitted, and Florence named as the place to which the Greeks should come : how the galleys of the Pope outstripped the galleys of the Council, and bore the Greeks in triumph from Constantinople to a town in the centre of Italy, where the Pope was all-powerful : how they were treated there : and why they were subsequently removed to Florence, would reveal a series of intrigues of the lowest order, if I had space to transcribe them ; unfortunately, they were too patent at every stage of the Council for the real objects of its promoters to admit of the slightest doubt. Between John Palæologus and Eugenius it was a barter of temporal and spiritual gains from first to last. One had his capital to guarantee from attack : the other his position in Italy to establish. Each hoped to be victorious through the other, Eugenius over the Basle fathers, Palæologus over the Turks. The more sailors and soldiers the Pope promised, the greater submission the Emperor engaged to extort from his bishops to the teaching of the Latin Church. Three cardinals solemnly notified to the Emperor what succours he might expect from the Pope when the union of the Churches had been accomplished, just as he had succeeded in getting all his bishops but one to declare for it. There would be ships and money to take them home : three hundred soldiers for the defence of their capital to be maintained there at the cost of the Pope. Two galleys would remain on guard there at his cost likewise. When the Emperor had need of ships of war, the Pope would supply twenty, and maintain them for him at his own expense for six months. And in case the Emperor should need help by land, the Pope, *by Christ*, would do his utmost to get Christian nations to send an army to his assistance." When union was imminent, the Emperor said : " The time draws near : we must be thinking of our departure." The Pope replied, " I have seen to it already and will see to it. I sent a captain all in good time to prepare ships, and should anything else be needed for your return, I will give orders for it at once : meanwhile, take this paper from me, and when you have read it, let me have your reply." *This was the definition ;* not, indeed, in the precise shape in which it passed : but ships and money were to be forthcoming when it was signed. Such were the preliminaries to the joint declaration of the two Churches on the Procession of the Holy Ghost, trans- lated literally from the Acts of the Council. Shall I avow it, my Lord ? my blood curdles as I transcribe them : but the worst is not told. Eugenius, the only Pope who ever presided over [such] a General Council in person, what does history say of his general character—of the holy zeal exhibited by him while the Council for re-uniting Christendom was sitting, or in conciliating adhesion

to it after it was over ?   One might have expected antecedently
that his presence and example would have influenced the Council,
as no other Council had ever been influenced before, for good.
" Eugenius," says his most partial biographer—I am quoting from
Ciaconius, " was esteemed constant in adhering to his engagements, *unless* he happened to have promised anything which it
were better to recal than to perform."   He was exchanging angry
censures and excommunications with the Council of Basle, all
the time that he affected to be promoting union at Florence with
all his might.   " Alas," exclaimed the great Archbishop of Pa-
lermo, one of his own cardinals subsequently, " what kind of
union will this turn out, fraught at its very commencement with
so much discord and scandal to the Latin Church ?"   Never were
forebodings more fully justified by the event.   Blondus, the
Pope's secretary, is lost in wonder at the vast sums of money
expended by his master in conciliating the high dignitaries or
indigent prelates of the Greek Emperor with *presents*—Syropulus,
one of the number, less scrupulously calls them bribes—and in
maintaining, *at no less cost, his own army simultaneously*, at the
head of which, operating against Nicholas Piccinino, Philip of
Milan, or Francis Sforza, petty chieftains of some rival factions,
was John Vitellius Vitelleschi, cardinal of Florence and Latin
patriarch of Alexandria.   Such were the interests to which the
Pope found time to attend, and such the ministers to whom he
consigned their execution, while the Council of Florence was
sitting.   Before the Council was over, Vitelleschi was suddenly
seized and put to death, without any trial, by his orders.   " Such
is the fickleness, and such are the vicissitudes of human affairs,"
says the cardinal's biographer, " that he who was treated to-day
with scorn and contumely, was two days before ordering
about everybody, and disposing of everything at pleasure, within
the domain of the Church ; governing Rome, the patrimony, the
duchy, Campania, the coast, and whatever else belonged to the
Church."   Let us hear who succeeded him.   Lewis, Archbishop
of Florence—the city in which the Council was still sitting—

Patriarch of Aquileia, *made cardinal*, we are expressly told, not for aught that he had done at the Council, but for having defeated in battle Nicholas Piccinino. " He," says his biographer, " *merited the love of Eugenius to that extent by his military prowess*, that he became first Bishop of Dalmatia, then Archbishop of Florence, finally Patriarch of Dalmatia, being the first Venetian who had ever held that See." Eugenius, a true-born Venetian, was fond of his race ; and when they had approved themselves good soldiers—anything, alas ! but the soldiers of Christ—they merited his exceeding love. The culminating distinction reserved for his fellow-townsman was to succeed the patriarch of Aquileia as commander-in-chief of the papal army ; and the first thought of the new patriarch of Aquileia on entering upon office was not to keep Eugenius to his engagements to the Greek Emperor of succouring him against the Turks, but to engage the Pope in hostilities against his own rival in adventure, Francis Sforza, whom from that time forth Eugenius, acting under the advice of his commander-in-chief, the archbishop, bent all his energies to crush, writing at the same time to Constantinople with the utmost assurance to tell Constantine Palæologus, the brother and heir of John, that it was the supineness of the Emperor in carrying out the terms of the union, and nothing else, that had delayed his fulfilling his engagements to him. The Greeks had agreed to the Florentine definition, and left Florence on the understanding that they might retain their own rites and their own Creed : it was not till Eugenius thought he could tell Europe that they had conformed *to the Roman rite*—we have this in his own words— that he condescended to aid them as he had promised : and even then, Hungary, not Constantinople, was his uppermost thought.

Such, therefore, we learn from history, was the conduct of the only Pope who ever sat at the head of a Council, all through the time when he was sitting and acting as such, in the only Council that ever met exclusively for re-uniting Christendom. Now, what guarantees have we, my Lord, or can we have, that the same conduct may not be displayed again, while the same system remains in full force? The personal holiness of the reigning pontiff may be some security while we are blessed with it, but it may be laid in the grave to-morrow: and against this, strong as it is, there is the undying system, which has always proved immeasurably stronger than any Pope, when its interests were threatened. Are there not papal Zouaves to be cared for as well as bishops, and papal territory to be thought of and battled for, as well as dogma? And have we never read of Pius IX. *himself* anxiously negotiating with a Protestant premier for a supply of 7,000 or 8,000 muskets of light calibre for his civic guard, which he thought imperative, but was unable to pay for, and unwilling to procure from "Naples, Turin, or Austria" just then?* Nobody would contend that Pius IX. was indebted to the system for his many virtues: and history shews that Eugenius could not have acted in most cases as he did, had it not been for the system. Therefore, by all who are praying and hoping for the re-union of Christendom in a corporate sense, Eugenius at the head of the Council of Florence cannot be scanned too closely. Look at his acts there in the practical light in which alone the men of this age will ever be disposed generally to regard them. Of what conceivable advantage can his presence be said to have been to the Council? Did it prevent hypocrisy, deceit, and secular intrigue from reigning there: rather was it not the prime cause of their reigning there, to the confusion of all the good and learned men on both sides? They prayed and argued to little purpose under such a head. Can his presence have been as much as a negative safeguard against error? This is probably the utmost that can be conceded: and even this admits of some question, at least as long as the proposition inserted in the definition at his instance remains unreconciled with history, or with previous dogma. Meanwhile, the main point in the controversy was never explained at all: though it had been waiting seven hundred years for a settlement. Policy, that was as old as the controversy, forbade this.

I pass from questions of Faith to questions of Morals,—for on

* Guizot's Last Days of Louis Philippe, p. 321.

both Rome claims to be infallible,—and once more I limit my criticisms to the Rome of the last 1000 years, and to her trustworthiness as a practical guide. How has duty to man—the *suum cuique* of political justice—fared at her hands ? What we have heard from S. Bernard already may help to determine this. "Abbots are exempted from bishops, bishops from archbishops, archbishops from primates or patriarchs. Can this be good in theory, can it be excused in practice ? Can you possibly think it lawful for you to dismember the Church, confound order, disturb the boundaries which your fathers have set ?" I used to estimate those words very differently ten or twelve years ago from what I do now. I used to consider S. Bernard and all other complainants of his stamp in the middle ages indirectly responsible for the evils which they denounced, as having consented in themselves or in their forefathers to the system out of which they flowed. That system could never have thriven, or become possessed of any coercive power, without their aid or acquiescence. The Papacy could never be said to have made conquest of mediæval Europe by force of arms. It took root, because the soil was congenial : its fruits were tasted, and found palatable. When it had been proved beneficial to the body politic in general, or rather incomparably better than anything else that offered to men then, it was encouraged by all. It had its abuses unquestionably : all honour to its supporters for their candour in denouncing them : still in estimating their language I could not honestly shut my eyes to the fact that they clung to the system under which they lived, were parties to it in practice, and never dreamt of exchanging it for another, thus proving that it existed in the main, abuses excepted, with their full concurrence. I also remembered that there were numbers amongst ourselves who could be eloquent on the evils of parliamentary government, and dwell forebodingly on the omnipotence of the House of Commons, without at all meaning to assert that any one of our constitutional changes had been brought about illegally, without in any sense wishing to go back to what we had been under the Tudors or Plantagenets.

Subsequent investigations have shewn me the one-sidedness of this explanation. It contemplated the West either as the whole Church, or else as competent to modify the discipline of the whole Church at will to suit its own predilections or well-being. S. Bernard, by his mention of patriarchs, had evidently travelled beyond the limits of the West for his facts. His words therefore —" Can you possibly think it lawful for you to *dismember the Church*, confound order, disturb the boundaries which your fathers had assigned them"—had a deeper and a wider meaning than I had assigned them formerly. He preferred a charge with which my ears had long been familiar in another application. The West had a perfect right to alter its own ecclesiastical polity, so far as the constitutions of the whole Church permitted. This was precisely the liberty claimed for themselves by the champions of the Church of England at the Reformation. But the West had no right at all, in legislating for itself, to innovate upon the existing and unrepealed ordinances of the whole Church. This was precisely the charge brought against the Church of England by the late Archdeacon Wilberforce, and which I for the time thought unanswerable. Therefore, admitting the allegations of S. Bernard to be true to the letter, with what face could I deny the Church of Rome to have been a much greater offender than the Church of England so far—a much greater offender, because, claiming to be the executive of the whole Church, she ought to have been the first to enforce, the last to contravene its existing statutes ? The question remained, how she had carried her point ? This, of course, S. Bernard could not have answered. The Church of England had taken advantage of the Reformation to carry hers, and a schism between her and Rome had been the consequence. I now asked how far the conduct of Rome in this respect could have contributed to the earlier schism between the East and West, and I am bound to say that history replied with twice the clearness and twice the sternness that it had previously replied in the case of the Creed. History deposed in short unhesitatingly that Rome rose to the eminence which she occupied in the thirteenth century when at her zenith—and from which in the Providence of God she has been gradually, but surely, descending ever since—most unrighteously, *as concerns the Church* —the whole Church I mean—by fraud and force : by the weapon of the weak, and the weapon of the strong, alternately put into her hand, and employed by her as legitimate, for the spread of her own power, to the dismemberment and destruction of the Church at large : the most striking specimens of each kind being the Pseudo-decretals, including of course the Pseudo-donation, and the Crusades. By these means, her bishop aspired to become Patriarch of the whole Church as well as Pope. I must find space for a few words upon each.

1. No certain proof, to the best of my belief, has been discovered as yet, that the pseudo-decretals and pseudo-donation were manufactured at Rome, or by order of Rome ; for all that, Rome stands committed to them no less than if she had done both, as we shall see. They purported to embody the formal teaching of her earliest pontiffs. She must have known from the first therefore, or been able to ascertain, whether they came from her archives or not : yet she studiously forebore from inquiring, and said nothing. It was enough for her that their genuineness came to be generally believed in, that they favoured her aggrandisement, and could be employed with decisive effect against those who contested it. She cared nothing for the palpable contradiction between them and the acknowledged Canons of the whole Church which she was bound to uphold and enforce. As this is just the point which has been eluded hitherto by the apologists of the pseudo-decretals, it will need unfolding at some length.

That what is called the " Code of the Universal Church " was in existence as a collection at the time of the fourth Council is established by Justellus and others indisputably from the manner in which a *book* of Canons was referred to there in the ninth and eleventh Actions, canons being in each case cited from it as the 83rd and 84th, 95th and 96th, according to the exact numbering which they bear there now. For the same reason it can have been no other collection that was authoritatively confirmed by the first Canon of the same Council in these words : " We pronounce it to be fit and just that the canons of the holy Fathers made in every synod to the present time be in full force."* To these subsequently the Council appended its own : all of which down to the 28th were passed unanimously : and this I omit on the ground that it was never confirmed by Rome, the old rule being, as we are told by Socrates, Sozomen, and Theodoret, all of them Greeks, that no canons could be passed without the consent of the Pope. The code of the Universal Church therefore down to this 28th Canon of Chalcedon is unquestionably binding on the whole Church still, and always has been, except in cases where it can be shewn to have been modified by subsequent legislation of equal authority. Now in this code there is no mention whatever of the See of Rome, as a supreme power, or even ultimate court of appeal, though its primacy is implied throughout. Hence when the subject of its appellate jurisdiction came before the heads of the African Church in the fifth century, among whom was S. Augustine, their deliberate finding, which they reported to the Pope, and on which they acted themselves, was, that " the Nicene decrees plainly committed both the inferior clergy and the bishops themselves to their own metropolitans : having most wisely and justly provided that all things shall be determined in the very places where they arise : for that the grace of the Holy Spirit will never be wanting in every province, whereby equity may be prudently discerned and constantly maintained by the ministers of Christ, especially when every man has liberty, if he be offended with the determination of his judges, to appeal to a provincial, or if need be to a general Council." The African bishops confine their remarks to the Nicene Canons, not feeling themselves under the circumstances called upon to examine more : but nobody who has studied the remaining canons comprised in this code could maintain that its regulations, on the

* I adopt Mr. Johnson's translations : *Vade Mecum*, vol. ii. p. 41, *et seq.*

subject of appeals, as it stood then, could have been stated more
fairly. Since then indeed the Sardican Canons authorising
bishops in extreme cases—and bishops alone—to appeal to the
Pope, which were then unknown to the African Church, have
been received in the East and West alike : yet against them we
must always remember is to be set the 9th Canon of the fourth
Council, and therefore one of this code to which Rome is bound
—allowing that " if any bishop or clergy should have a dispute
with their metropolitan, they may apply to the exarch of their
diocese, or else to the throne of Constantinople, and have their
case tried there.* More persons are thus authorised in this
code to appeal to the See of Constantinople than in the Sardican
Canons themselves to Rome. And except on this one subject of
appeal, jurisdiction in all its branches is both explicitly and
rigorously restricted to the local boundaries in force then, and
never to be enlarged. The consent of Rome to the 28th Canon
of Chalcedon was emphatically refused and persistently withheld
on these grounds. The 2nd Canon of Constantinople is to
this day a standing witness against the See in whose interests the
28th of Chalcedon was framed: " Let not bishops go out of their
diocese to churches out of their bounds : but let the bishop of
Alexandria, according to the Canon, administer the affairs of
Egypt, and the bishops of the East the affairs of the East only,
with a salvo to the ancient privileges of the Church of Antioch
mentioned in the Nicene Canons. . . . And let not bishops go out
of their dioceses to ordinations, or any administration, unless
they be invited. And by the aforesaid Canon concerning dioceses
being observed it is evident that the provincial synod will have
the management of every province, as was decreed at Nicæa.
The Churches amongst the barbarians must be governed according
to the customs which prevailed with their ancestors."
This Canon was occasioned by the irregular proceedings of the
Patriarch of Alexandria ; it may be said to embody the spirit of
the whole code. Another Canon, the 8th of Ephesus, occasioned

* The 17th Canon is to the same effect.

by the attempts of the Patriarch of Antioch upon the independence of Cyprus, is not less worth our attention and runs as follows:—" Our fellow-bishop Reginus, beloved by God, and Zeno and Evagrius, most religious bishops of the province of Cyprus, with him, have publicly declared an innovation contrary to the ecclesiastical laws, and the Canons of the holy Fathers, *and which touches the liberty of all.* . . . The holy General Synod hath therefore decreed that the rights of every province formerly, and from the beginning, belonging to it be preserved clear and inviolable, and that ancient custom prevail : every metropolitan having power to take copies of the things now transacted for his own security. *But if any one introduce a regulation contrary to the present determination, the holy General Synod decrees that it be of no force.*"

To that extent were the Fathers of the Third Council persuaded that unity in the Church would be much more imperilled by superseding ancient and immemorial rights to secure system, than by leaving a few isolated bishops here and there independent of any ecclesiastical superior, and " autocephali," to discourage innovation. I pass straight from these canons to the pseudo-decretals and pseudo-donation,* that the contrast between them may be seen more readily. For instance, S. Anacletus in an encyclic addressed to the faithful is made to say :—" Should more difficult questions arise, or should the case be one of high importance, or concern bishops of high standing, let them be referred, in case of appeal, to the Apostolic See ; for this the *Apostles appointed by command of our Lord,* that all greater and more arduous questions should be brought before the Apostolic See on which Christ founded His universal Church." And again : " The Apostolic See was appointed by the Lord, and no one else, head and hinge of all the Churches : and as a door is swayed by its hinge, so, by disposal of the Lord, all Churches are swayed as this holy See may dispose." Or, as Constantine in his pseudo-donation is supposed to have decreed, " We decree and ordain

* Migne's Patrol., vol. cxxx.

that it—the Roman See—should have dominion as well over the four principal Sees of Alexandria, Antioch, Jerusalem, and Constantinople, as over all the Churches of God in the whole earth besides : and that its pontiff for the time being should be superior and prince of all the world, and all things necessary to be ordained for the worship of God, or for the faith of Christians, to be regulated by his judgment.''

Where have we a syllable, my Lord, of all this in the genuine code of the Church : and can it be gainsaid for a moment to which of these two theories of jurisdiction—that of the pseudo-decretals, or that of the code—the development of the Papacy was due, or that it was not effected literally by ''disturbing the boundaries assigned by the fathers,'' as S. Bernard says, among which are, conspicuously, the canons to which I have called attention? If the universal jurisdiction claimed by the Roman Pontiff in the middle ages was not based on the authority of the pseudo-decretals, why were they so constantly cited in its support? Where is the law of the whole Church that either attests or sanctions it ?

Local synods and local churches cannot undertake to legislate for the whole Church, much less repeal what the whole Church has ordained. Concordats with kings, à fortiori, can do neither. Is it credible, that the Papacy should have so often appealed to these forgeries for its extended claims, had it any better authorities—distinctive authorities—to fall back upon ? Every disputant on the Latin side finds in these forgeries a convincing argument against the Greeks. ''To prove this,'' the universal jurisdiction of the Pope, said Abbot Barlaam, himself converted by them from the Greek Church, to convert his countrymen— ''one need only look through the decretal epistles of the Roman Pontiffs from S. Clement to S. Silvester.'' In the twenty-fifth session of the Council of Florence the provincial of the Dominicans is ordered to address the Greeks on the rights of the Pope, the Pope being present. Twice he argues from the pseudo-decretal of S. Anacletus : at another time from a synodical letter

of S. Athanasius to Felix : at another time from a letter of
Julius to the Easterns : all forgeries. Afterwards, in reply to
objections taken by Bessarion, in conference, to their authority,
apart from any question of their authenticity, his position in
another speech is "that *those decretal epistles of the Popes*
being synodical epistles in each case, are entitled to the same
authority as the canons themselves." Can we need further
evidence of the weight attached to them on the Latin side ?
Popes appealed to them in their official capacity as well as private
doctors. Leo IX. for instance, to the pseudo-donation in the
prolix epistle written by him, or in his name, to Michael Ceru-
larius, Patriarch of Constantinople, on the eve of the schism.
Eugenius IV. to the pseudo-decretals of S. Alexander and Julius,
during the negotiations for healing it, in his instructions to the
Armenians. But why, my Lord, need I travel any further for
proofs, when in the Catechism of the Council of Trent, that has
been for three centuries the accredited instructor of the clergy
themselves, recommended authoritatively by so many Popes,
notwithstanding the real value of these miserable impostures
having been for three centuries before the world—I find these
words :* " On the Primacy of the Supreme Pontiff, see the third
epistle (that is, pseudo-decretal) of Anacletus " ! Such is,
actually, the authority to which the clergy of our own days are
referred, *in the first instance,* for sound and true views on the
Primacy ; afterwards, when they have mastered what is said
there, they may turn to three more authorities, all culled likewise from Gratian, which they will not fail to interpret in accordance with the ideas they have already imbibed. Nor can I refrain
from calling attention to a much more flagrant case. On the
Sacrament of Confirmation there had been many questions raised
by the Reformers calculated to set people thinking, and anxious
to know the strict truth respecting it. On this, the Catechism
proceeds as follows :†

"Since it has been already shewn how necessary it would be

* De Ord. Sacram., § 49.   † § 5.

to teach generally respecting all the Sacraments, by whom they were instituted, so there is need of similar instruction respecting Confirmation, that the faithful may be the more attracted by the holiness of this Sacrament. Pastors must therefore explain that not only was Christ our Lord the author of it, but that, on the authority of the Roman Pontiff S. Fabian (the pseudo-decretal attributed to him, that is), He instituted the rite of the chrism, and the words used by the Catholic Church in its administration."

Strange phenomenon indeed, that the asseverations of such authorities should be still ordered to be taught as Gospel from our pulpits in these days, when everybody that is acquainted with the merest rudiments of ecclesiastical history knows how absolutely unauthenticated they are in point of fact, and how unquestionably the authorities cited to prove them are forgeries. Even Estius says, "*Plerique opinantur Apostolos in conferendo confirmationis sacramento, chrismate nunquam usos fuisse,*" though in his day men still believed in the genuineness of the pseudo-decretals. Absolutely, my Lord, with such evidence before me, I am unable to resist the inference that truthfulness is not one of the strongest characteristics of the teaching of even the modern Church of Rome: for is not this a case palpably where its highest living authorities are both indifferent to having possible untruths preached from the pulpit, and something more than indifferent to having forgeries, after their detection as such, adduced from the pulpit to authenticate facts? Jealous enough they may be that what they teach should be believed as true : that it should be in strict accordance with actual truth is another point, to which with the evidence before me I must suppose them callous. This, again, strongly reminds me of a conversation I had with the excellent French priest who received me into the Roman Catholic Church some time subsequently to that event. I had as an Anglican inquired very laboriously into the genuineness of the "Santa Casa : " and having visited Nazareth and Loretto since, and plunged into the question anew at each place, came back more thoroughly convinced than ever of its utterly fictitious character, notwithstanding the privileges bestowed on it by so many Popes. On stating my convictions to him, his only reply was : "There are many things in the Breviary which I do not believe myself." Oh ! the stumbling-blocks of a system in the construction of which forgeries have been so largely used, in which it is still thought possible for the clergy to derive edification from legends which they cannot believe, and the people instruction from works of acknowledged imposture ! Let us hope that this will be one of the very first questions ventilated at the ensuing Council.

2. A few words on the Crusades, and I sum up. My thesis is that they completed the ecclesiastical aggrandisement of the Papacy by force. Various judgments have been formed of them from their having a social and political, as well as ecclesiastical side, from their having been espoused by so many good as well as bad men, from their having been commenced in enthusiasm though they ended in crime. But view them in what light we please, they could never have taken place without the Pope, and therefore, for good or for evil, he stands committed to them in every sense. Now even socially and politically, I contend they were productive of much greater calamity to mankind than good, but ecclesiastically beyond dispute they entailed as much ruin on the Religion and Church of Christ as the worst that has ever befallen either under the Turks. Socially, they carried but little religion or virtue with them into the East apart from chivalry : which those who remained there soon lost from tyrannising over those whom they had come to set free : while those who returned deluged Europe with their vices. Very different were the commodities imported into Europe by the fugitive Greeks from Constantinople when it fell under the Turks. Merchants, peacefully trading with the East, would have supplied our ancestors with all the real improvements supposed to have been derived through the Crusades, at less crime by half. Politically, the Crusades proved a fatal mistake for humanity, let alone true religion. It has been often set to the credit of the Popes that they saved Europe from

the Turks. History says that they opened the door by which the Turks came in. It is certain that the Latins proved the ruin of the Greek Empire much more than the Turks. Had the Greek Empire been left to itself, or helped honestly, it would have barred the Turks from Europe to this day, and preserved all the civilization, population, and Christianity contained in it for man. But ecclesiastically, that is, in the province of all others appertaining to the Popes as Heads of the Church, I can discover no redeeming feature whatever in the Crusades from first to last. The combination of the cross with the sword demoralised all orders alike. Under their influence Christian bishops became generals of armies and shedders of blood in hand-to-hand conflicts with spear and shield. What was attempted by all after their first burst of enthusiasm was over, was to subjugate the Churches of the East to that of Rome in a way opposed to the canons immemorially and universally received by the Church. The Easterns were trampled upon for maintaining their rights, ejected from their churches as far as was possible, and supplanted by a rival hierarchy wherever the Crusaders conquered. The researches of the late Sir Francis Palgrave go far to prove that they actually set out with this object : some of the first letters written home by them to the Pope who organised them shew, at all events, that the idea dawned upon them with their first success. "As for the Turks," say they, "and Pagans, we have overcome them : but the heretical Greeks and Armenians, Syrians and Jacobities, we cannot overcome. Only come over to us, and complete that which you have commenced with us, and the whole world will obey you."* Now this was exactly what Innocent III. completed on the capture of Constantinople by the Franks and Venetians. Of all breaches of the canons in ecclesiastical history, it would be difficult to find one more flagrant than the act of Innocent in consecrating Morosini Patriarch of Constantinople, his own "venerable brother," as he had styled him but a short time before, John Camater, the rightful pa-

* Baluz. Miscel. iii. 60, ed. Mansi.

triarch, being alive, and expelled by force, without any previous trial or inquiry. The excuse for Innocent is that he believed in the genuineness of the pseudo-decretals, and was acting in accordance with other established precedents of might made right. But his own letters testify to a mind in perpetual conflict between his own better feelings and the requirements of his office. He had excommunicated the Venetians already for having invaded Christian territory : he is subsequently found accepting their conquests, and with his own hands consecrating their nominee. What a plight for one calling himself Head of the Church to be reduced to by his worldly ties ! To have to consent to the desolation by fire and sword of what was then infinitely the largest and most flourishing part of the Church by the other in contempt of his own orders : to look on while the ancient landmarks of the Church were one after another uptorn by violence : and then, by accepting a share of the spoils himself, to identify not himself merely but his See for ever, with the outrageousness of the whole proceeding ! What frightful hy-pocrisy, what downright profanity for this ever to have been designated a Crusade, a holy war, a war waged in behalf of the life-giving Cross ! Who can possibly believe in a God of justice, and doubt His holding the Papacy heavily responsible for all this ?

My Lord, there is a solemn document before the world—I may say one of the solemnest—addressed to us all without exception, of which the meanest is therefore justified in requesting explanations, should it contain anything hard to be understood, or beyond his ken. I confine my request to the following passage : " Known unto all are the unwearied cares wherewith the Roman pontiffs have laboured to defend the deposit of faith, the discipline of the clergy, and their education in sanctity and doctrine, as well as the holiness and dignity of the matrimonial state, have promoted more and more the Christian education of both sexes, and have studied to provide for and to cherish religion, piety, and good morals : to defend justice, and the tranquillity, order, and prosperity of civil society." If this assertion is to be understood *de jure*, as a declaration of what the Roman pontiffs ought to have done in all ages, nothing could be more true : but if *de facto*, as a declaration of what they have done for the last thousand years, the history of the Crusades alone would suffice to determine the extent to which the reverse is more true. Further comment is needless.

What, then, are the conclusions ensuing from the facts which have been adduced ? First, that although Rome may have never erred from the Faith in point of dogma, she has trifled with it on one point in practice so often for the last thousand years, that her conduct has been a stumbling-block to others, and occasioned a division of the Eastern and Western Churches on doctrinal grounds. Secondly, that by allowing the primitive code of the Church to be stealthily supplanted by a new code based upon forgeries, which she herself accepted without examination, and endeavoured to make binding upon others by violence, she has occasioned a division of the Eastern and Western Churches on disciplinary grounds : in other words, that it is to the flagrant unfaithfulness and injustice of her governmental policy, both as regards doctrine and discipline, that secession from her Communion has been, and is still, due.

I am not aware that any demur to this conclusion, in theory, can be raised even by maximisers. But I will begin with what I trust I may designate without offence the high orthodox. In a Review, stated on its title-page to be " Par les Pères de la Compagnie de Jesus," and therefore committing the whole Society to its contents, I read, exactly two years ago this month, as follows, in a paper on the pseudo-decretals.* " Cette nouvelle discipline "—that of the pseudo-decretals, what he had just called "*la réforme pseudo-Isidorienne ! ! !*—était bonne assurement." It would have been difficult for the writer to have said otherwise, for the reasons he gives—" Adoptée par S. Nicholas en 865, par le huitième concile œcumenique en 870 "—not received by the East—

* Etudes Religieuses, No. 47, p. 392.

" *confirmée par le concile de Trent en* **1564**, *elle est depuis neuf siècles le droit commun dans l'Eglise Catholique.*" ! ! ! Have I said more than this, namely, that our existing system *originated* with, and is *based* on, the pseudo-decretals ? To his infinite credit, the writer adds, " Mais l'ancienne discipline était bonne aussi, puisque, pendant les huit premiers siècles, l'Eglise n'en avait point connu d'autre . . . La nouvelle discipline pouvait par conséquent être utile : elle n'était point nécessaire. Ce qu'il est impossible de justifier et même d'excuser, c'est le moyen employé par le pseudo-Isidore pour arriver à ses fins. Le mensonge demeure toujours un mal, même lorsque celui qui en use se propose un bien. *Non faciamus mala ut veniant bona.* Et que l'on ne vienne pas nous dire : il n'y a pas un imposture, mais seulement malentendu. Que l'on ne rejette pas la méprise, *dont le monde Chrétien à été la dupe pendant sept siècles,* sur un concours de circonstances indépendantes de la volonté du pseudo-Isidore. Non, il y a eu de sa part mensonge prémédité." In fine: " Les fausses décrétals *n'ont produit que du mal.*" Aye, but whose business was it to see that Christendom should not have been duped and damaged in this way, and to have said " non possumus" a thousand times before they allowed it, instead of becoming active parties to it themselves ? However, it is admitted on all hands that Popes may make " *serious mistakes*" as Church-governors. " To every Pope," said the *Dublin Review,* in July last, " appertains the office on the one hand of teaching the Church : on the other hand, of ruling and piloting her. It is admitted by all Catholics without exception that a Pope may make serious mistakes in exercising this latter office, though they well know that on the whole he obtains most special assistance of the Holy Ghost in its execution." Certainly, nothing but " the most special assistance of the Holy Ghost" could have prevented their " serious mistakes" from becoming more serious, or overruled the effects of their misrule so as to exhibit the entire dialogue between our Lord and S. Peter on a well-known occasion, interpreted by the light of events in the clearest manner. Doc-

trinal inerrancy was promised by our Lord to S. Peter, standing
at the head, and speaking in the name, of all the Apostles, in
reply to a question addressed to them all, and not to him alone.
His successors, down to the President of the Council of Florence
himself, have acknowledged, as I shall point out presently, that
they have never spoken in the name of the whole Church *since
the schism.* The very first time S. Peter essayed teaching on his
own judgment, *after his confession,* and apart from the rest, he
was told by our Lord authoritatively : " Thou savourest not the
things that be of God, but those that be of men." The other
Apostles, therefore, had they followed or upheld him in what he
then taught, would have done wrong. In the same way, admitting all the doctrinal inerrancy possessed by S. Peter to have been
bequeathed by him to his successors, as it has not plainly preserved them from allowing the Creed of the Church to be interpolated at the will of kings uncanonically : from upholding
forgeries as authentic testimony : from perpetrating the most
iniquitous acts themselves, under cover of their authority, and
citing them in proof of some of the gravest points in their own
distinctive teaching respecting the Sacraments, unsupported by
other testimony, it cannot follow from the mere possession of
this gift by them ever so completely, that corporate union with
Rome can never be maintained too dearly, or that disunion with
Rome may never have been a duty. The Popes are not to be
followed where they have erred, any more than S. Peter : therefore, when they made fellowship with their errors indispensable
to fellowship with their See, so that one could not be maintained
without the other, the only course left was to abandon both.
Unerring faith is necessary for the Church, but it is not all that
is necessary—honesty, justice, truthfulness, meekness, and self-
denial, are among the determining principles that bind Christians
together, as well as their faith. Unerring faith must govern in
conformity with all these, or it must cease to govern. It cannot
bear its possessor harmless for moral obliquities of what kind
soever in the conduct of the body politic : it will but serve to

enhance the guilt of its possessor, like the prophetic gift of the high-priest who condemned Christ; and ceasing to govern, it must cease to speak, for it is tied to speak at the head and in the name of the whole body. The lungs are in the body, though the mouth is in the head : therefore, when separated, neither can utter in the same sense as when united : not that their separation need in the corporate sense be fatal to their vitality. Every truth which they had enunciated infallibly when united might be retained equally by both after they had parted company, and both might be preserved from error in their isolation by a special providence, till their re-union. Both too might speak, and speak the truth equally, but what they said would not be beyond question or revision. It might prove as true as any of the most infallible truths ever promulgated, but not having the promise of infallibility attached to it under the circumstances under which it was uttered, it would require that plenary confirmation which union alone can ensure.

This theory, besides harmonising with facts which it is impossible to gloss over or dispute, receives additional countenance from the action as well as the language of the Popes since the schism, and explains existing phenomena much more reasonably, as I shall hope to shew, than any other. In general, the action of Rome has been prompt, peremptory, and decisive, almost to a fault ; bold almost to rashness ; unhesitating almost to arrogance : she seems intent on impressing people with nothing so much as her own self-sufficiency : her utter inability to commit a mistake of any kind, or be in the wrong. Contrast this with her extraordinary shiftiness and indecision on the two Creeds, the old and the interpolated. When has she ever affirmed them to be doctrinally the same : what, according to her, is the exact difference between their respective professions on the Procession ? As to their use, we can only go back to ground already traversed. Leo III. forbade the use of the interpolated form. His successors winked at it, and ended by adopting it themselves : still, they doubted about enforcing it on those who clung to the old form. Gregory X.

read the letters of the Easterns at the Second Council of Lyons, begging to be excused using the interpolated Creed, without answering them : but the Creed was thrice chanted there in that form exclusively notwithstanding. Innocent V., who succeeded him, was imperative that the "*Filioque*" clause " should not be omitted on any account by them in chanting the Creed." Nicholas III. went further, and added that " as unity of faith could not consist with diversity in those that professed . . . therefore, the desire of the Roman Church was, that it should be chanted uniformly with the additional clause by the Greeks as well as the Latins." This was, in effect, deciding that the old form of the Creed should be superseded : but it was never carried out. When the subject was revived at the Council of Florence, Rome was more diplomatic than she had ever been previously. No Creed at all was recited there : nor was any hint dropped whether both forms conjointly, or one without the other, should be considered the Creed of the Church. These various policies having to be reconciled with each other, it was at length ruled by Clement VIII. and Benedict XIV. successively : "*Græci credere tenentur etiam a Filio Spiritum S. procedere, sed non tenentur pronuntiare, nisi subesset scandalum.*" I am indebted to you, my Lord, for directing my attention to this position more particularly. Let us see how it would have read in the mouth of S. Athanasius. " *Ariani credere tenentur Filium Homousion esse cum Patre, sed non tenentur pronuntiare, nisi subesset scandalum.*" The Alexandrine fathers, A.D. 362, under S. Athanasius, probably went greater lengths in condescendence than any Council before or since : but to the extent of allowing the Nicene Creed to be recited by heretics without the very word inserted in it to confound their heresy, Pope Liberius himself, had he been present, could not have induced them to go ; What then ? Were Clement VIII. and Benedict XIV. either of them disposed to be lukewarm with heresy ? I think not. The true meaning of their decision must be that in their inmost souls they were far from considering the Greeks heretics. How, indeed, could they, seeing that at the Council of Florence the representatives of the Eastern Church sat, debated, and subscribed on the same terms as the Western ? There had also been a passage in the original decree passed at Basle for inviting them thither, deliberately cancelled, because the word "heretics" or "dissenters" had crept into it unawares, as was said, in speaking of the Greeks. Further, on what grounds had the Councils of Lyons and Florence themselves been summoned? As Gregory X. puts it:—"Because of his extreme bitterness in beholding the rent of the Universal Church foreshadowed in the net of Peter the fisherman, that *brake* for the multitude of fishes which it enclosed : we do not say divided as regards its faith . . . but notoriously and lamentably divided as regards its faithful members." Or, as Eugenius IV. told his envoys : " It is for the union of the Western and Eastern Church, so long and ardently desired by us, that you are sent ; " or, as he told the Greeks when he despaired of union : " In what shall we be benefitted if we fail to unite the Church of God ?" * It was in strictest conformity with this view that the Council of Florence was to have been accepted on both sides, had it succeeded, as the Eighth Œcumenical Council : the title under which its acts were literally first published in Latin, A.D. 1526, in the Pontificate of Clement VII., and under which Cardinal Pole still speaks of it in his work of so much interest to us all, " The Reformation of England," dated Lambeth, 1556. And now, in our own days, there is the Letter Apostolic of Pius IX. " to the bishops of the Churches of the Eastern Rite " not in communion with him, containing the following sentence, of which the ink is scarce dry :—" We conjure you to come to this General Council, *as your predecessors came to the Second Council of Lyons*, held by the blessed Gregory, our predecessor of venerated memory, *and to the Council of Florence*, celebrated by our predecessor of happy memory, Eugenius IV.: that, thus renewing the bonds of ancient affection, and recalling to life that ancient peace, the heavenly and blessed gift of Christ, which in the course

---

* I have collected many more such passages in Part II. of my book, v. pp. 259—61, and 337—40.

of ages has become lost to us, we may make the serene brightness of longed-for union shine resplendent before all, after being sadly clouded, and after the painful darkness of long-lived discussion.''

If the Easterns are invited to come to this General Council as their predecessors came to the Councils of Lyons and Florence, the inference is inevitable that his present Holiness equally throws himself into the sentiments of his predecessors, and adopts their language. That is to say, Pius IX. beholds, and has acted on beholding, the same spectacle that caused Gregory X. so much anguish—the rent of the Universal Church foreshadowed in the net of Peter the fisherman, that brake . . . not, indeed, divided as regards its faith . . . but notoriously and lamentably divided as regards its faithful members : and his object at the forthcoming Council will be what Eugenius IV. assured the Greeks his was, "to unite the Church of God" in that sense. Therefore, not less inevitably, the formal teaching of the Popes, ever since the schism began till now, has been that the Church *is divided* as regards her members, and that there are Churches forming part of the Catholic Church, which are, and have been for ages, out of communion with their See. The Popes, indeed, have never practically said this of any Churches but the Eastern, and of the Eastern but those communicating with the Patriarch of Constantinople ; still, in admitting thus much, they most unquestionably concede that what we call the Roman Catholic Church has not constituted the whole Church, nor they themselves consequently spoken at the head of the whole Church, since the schism. To an impartial observer it would appear as though they were far from feeling easy themselves under the circumstances : far from certain, that if their title-deeds were examined into, their *de facto* position might not be shaken : unable to divest themselves of the idea that the Easterns had not been wholly to blame for withdrawing from their Communion, nor were chargeable with heresy for withholding their assent to the adoption of the " *Filioque* " clause. Else, why not have summoned a General Council long since to condemn them as heretics, instead of inviting them to a General Council again and again to discuss doctrine under their presidency ?

To the West, where they ruled by patriarchal as well as papal right, they might well be supposed to have adopted a more confident tone since the Reformation ; but the closer it is scrutinised the further it is seen to be from unhesitating and decisive. Those who had renounced their Communion were invited to the Council of Trent not to be condemned, but to be heard. If Luther was excommunicated twice, the Confession of Augsburg has never as yet been anathematised : if Queen Elizabeth was deposed, the Council of Trent had abstained deliberately from affirming that the bishops who had been consecrated in her reign and at her bidding were no bishops. Even the Thirty-nine Articles escaped censure. Hence, ever since the Council of Trent separated until now, attempts have been made continually, whether successful or not, to reconcile the Confession of Augsburg and the Thirty-nine Articles with its decrees. Anglican Orders, if they have not been recognised in practice, have never been declared invalid, still less the grounds of their invalidity set forth. It might be said that all this has been the effect of moderation and paternal tenderness on the part of the Popes : there can be little doubt that it has commended itself to their policy; still, as one of the most warmly debated points in modern times has been the power of the Popes and their true relation to the Church, who can fail to be struck with the absence of any formal assertion on their part that the terms "Catholic" and "Roman Catholic" are strictly convertible— with the fact that they have never striven to appropriate the term "Catholic," pure and simple, to their own Communion, but have commonly called it themselves, and been content that it should be called by others, the Roman-Catholic Church, as being its strict and adequate title. No doubt they have never failed to assert the doctrine of their own headship by divine right over the whole Church in the strongest terms, and the teaching of all those who obey them has always been that the Catholic Church has a visible Head upon earth, under Christ, called the Pope :

still all such teaching, read by the light of their own admissions respecting the Eastern Church, is seen to be but a declaration of what ought to be, not of what is : a picture of the ideal or of the primitive, not of the actually existing Church.   Where, indeed, is the part of Christendom seriously purporting to call itself the Catholic Church in these days? Roman-Catholic, Anglo-Catholic, Episcopal, Orthodox, or Presbyterian, all in their degree seem influenced by some hidden spell to abstain from arrogating to themselves or attributing to each other the epithet of "Catholic" without qualification, as it is applied to the Church in the Creed. Test existing phenomena by this theory, and the results are plain and straightforward.   One of its logical results would be that the administration of the Christian Sacraments might be frequented with profit outside the pale of the Roman Communion.   Is this confirmed by experience ?   My Lord, my own experience, which is confined to the single Communion in which you formerly bore office, that of the Church of England, says emphatically that it is : and there is no canon or ordinance that I know of forbidding me to maintain it.   You have preceded me yourself in expatiating on the workings of the Holy Spirit in the Church of England with your accustomed eloquence, and have not hesitated to attribute to its members many graces in virtue of the Sacrament of Baptism which you allow they administer on the whole validly : but there you stop.   I feel morally constrained to go further still.   If I had to die for it, I could not possibly subscribe to the idea that the Sacraments to which I am admitted week after week in the Roman Communion—Confession and the Holy Eucharist, for instance—confer any graces, any privileges, essentially different from what I used to derive from those same Sacraments, frequented with the same dispositions, in the Church of England. On the contrary, I go so far as to say, that comparing one with another strictly, some of the most edifying communions that I can remember in all my life were made in the Church of England, and administered to me by some that have since submitted to be re-ordained in the Church of Rome ; a ceremony, therefore, which, except as qualifying them to undertake duty there, I must consider superfluous. Assuredly, so far as the registers of my own spiritual life carry me, I have not been able to discover any greater preservatives from sin, any greater incentives to holiness, in any that I have received since : though, in saying this, I am far from intending any derogation to the latter. I frequent them regularly : I prize them exceedingly : I have no fault to find with their administration or their administrators in general. All that I was ever taught to expect from them they do for me, due allowance being made for my own shortcomings. Only I cannot possibly subscribe to the notion of my having been a stranger to their beneficial effects till I joined the Roman Communion, and I deny that it was my faith alone that made them what they were to me before then, unless it is through my faith alone that they are what they are to me now. Holding myself that there are realities attaching to the Sacraments of an objective character, I am persuaded, and have been more and more confirmed in this conviction as I have grown older, that the Sacraments administered in the Church of England are realities, objective realities, to the same extent as any that I could now receive at your hands : so that you yourself therefore consecrated the Eucharist as truly when you were Vicar of Lavington as you have ever done since. This may or may not be your own belief : but you shall be one of my foremost witnesses to its credibility, for I am far from basing it on the experiences of my own soul. My Lord, I have always been accustomed to look upon the Sacraments as so many means of grace, and to estimate their value, not by the statements of theologians, but by their effects on myself, my neighbours, and mankind at large. And the vast difference between the moral tone of society in the Christian and the pagan worlds I attribute not merely to the superiority of the rule of life prescribed in the Gospels, but to the inherent grace of the Sacraments enabling and assisting us to keep it to the extent we do. Taking this principle for my guide, I have been engaged constantly since I joined the Roman Communion in instituting comparisons between members of the Church of England and members of the Church of Rome generally, and between our former and our present selves in particular; or between Christianity in England and on the Continent; and the result in each case has been to confirm me in the belief which I have expressed already, that the notion of the Sacraments exercising any greater influence upon the heart and life in the Church of Rome than in the Church of England, admitting the dispositions of those who frequent them to be the same in both cases, is not merely preposterous, but as contrary both to faith and fact as is the opinion that the Pope is Antichrist and the Man of Sin. My Lord, there is no person in his sober senses who could affirm that you, for instance, began to be a devout, earnest, intelligent follower of Christ, an admirable master of the inner and the hidden life, a glorious example of self-sacrifice, a deep expounder of revealed mysteries and Gospel truths, when you embraced the Roman Communion; or that all those graces which you exhibited previously in the sight of men could be deduced from the one rite which you received unconsciously as a child, counteracted by all the bad and unwholesome food on which, according to this hypothesis, you must have lived ever afterwards. In the same way there is no ordinary person in his sober senses who could affect to discover any fundamental change for the better in you, morally or religiously, now from what you were then. There are some, on the contrary, to my knowledge, of your existing flock who profess that they have not half the liking for the sermons which they hear you deliver as Archbishop of Westminster that they have for the dear old volumes which you published as Archdeacon of Chichester, as fresh and full of fragrance to their instincts as ever. And I have heard the same said of another, whose parochial sermons, hailed as a masterpiece on their first appearance, have just burst forth into a second spring. People say that the sermons which *ci-devant* Anglican clergymen of note preached formerly read so much more natural than any that they have since delivered from Roman Catholic pulpits. They argued impartially, then, as men whose sole desire it was both to get at the truth, and uphold it at any cost : they never feared looking facts in the face, and were as little given to exaggerate those that made for them, as to keep out of sight or evade by subterfuge those which they could neither excuse nor explain. They were never tired of confessing their own sins or shortcomings. In a word, their tone was frank, honest, and manly. Now, they may preach with the same energy, but it is as though they preached under constraint or dictation. Either they are high-flown and exaggerated : or else punctilious and reserved : weighing each word as if they were repeating a task : always artificial, never themselves : as if committed to a thesis, which they must defend at all risks, and to which all facts must be accommodated, or else denied. Hence, do what they will, there is a distinction between themselves and the cause they advocate, which cannot fail to strike the most ordinary listener ; their words no longer carry the moral argument (ἠθικὴ πίστις) with them that they once did even among their followers : and the judgment of public opinion on them is that they are vapid and destitute of force by comparison. What people say of those generally who have become Roman Catholics in England of late years, is that they have deteriorated as a body rather than advanced. The foremost of them have not progressed in any perceptible degree—perceptible by others, that is—beyond the high standard to which they had attained before, as their lives, their writings, and their sermons testified : others, every allowance being made for the peculiar trials to which they have been subjected, have notoriously descended to a lower level of Christianity since they became Roman Catholics, from that in which they had been working previously ; and some have been driven from their moorings—in appearance at least— altogether. All this I hear said : and as far as my own experience goes, it is quite true : and for the life of me I cannot infer anything else from it than that sacramental grace is equally derivable from the same ordinances in both Communions, according to the dispositions of those who frequent them, and is not more indefectible in the one than the other. What I have seen of Roman Catholics myself, since joining their Church, all points to the same conclusion. Till then, I knew them only by report, which, founded on prejudice, was far from being in their favour : and I was horrified to find how shamefully it had misrepresented them. I found them—I mean the educated classes—all that in a general estimate members of a Christian Church should be : God-serving, charitable, conscientious, refined, intelligent : and I could discover nothing idolatrous or superstitious in their worship, nor anything at variance with first principles in their daily life. At home or abroad I was equally surprised to find them so different from what my traditional informants had described them, with so much to admire where I had supposed there was so much to reprobate. But afterwards—when my first emotions consequent on this discovery had subsided—when I came to ask myself the question, are these, then, the only true Christians that you have ever known in life : and till you conversed with them, had you never conversed with a true Christian before ? I can scarce describe the recoil that it occasioned in me ! Why my own father and mother would have compared with the best of them in all the virtues ordinarily possessed by Christians living in the world and discharging their duties conscientiously towards God and their neighbours, in, through, and for Christ. " All for Jesus" was as much their motto as it could be of any parents in Christendom : and well indeed would it be for all Roman Catholic children if they were blessed with no worse fathers and mothers than mine. Then I have, or have had, relatives and friends in numbers, members of the Church of England, whose homes I will undertake to say are to all intents and purposes as thoroughly Christian as any to be found elsewhere : and it would be sheer affectation or hypocrisy in me were I to pretend the contrary : or else to claim for my own friends and relatives any peculiar excellence distinguishing them from average specimens of the Anglican body. For a calm, unpresuming, uniform standard of practical Christianity, I

E

have seen nothing as yet amongst ourselves in any country superior to that of the English parsonage and its surroundings : go where I will, I am always thrown back upon one of these as the most perfect ideal of a Christian family : a combination amongst its members of the highest intelligence with the most unsullied purity and earnest faith I ever witnessed on earth. It was a privilege to have witnessed it. It was not far from Brackley. You may have known several such yourself. On describing the "daily round" of Christian life in the English Church—such as I had been accustomed to from a child—to the excellent priest who received me into communion on the Continent—our family prayers, our grace before and after meals, our readings of the Scriptures, our observance of Sunday, our services at Church, our Sunday schools—what did he do but mount his pulpit the Sunday following, and embodying all that I had told him in a fervid discourse, expatiate to a fashionable congregation in Paris on the many lessons of piety which they had to learn from their separated brethren on the other side of the Channel. " Such, too, was our general practice," he said to me in a private conversation, " before the Revolution : and we hope to recover it : but as yet there are few families where it exists." Of my countrymen he observed, " Leur bonne foi est acceptée pour leur vraie foi." I took this explanation on trust at the time, but have since given it up as inadequate. For if it be said that faith and integrity of purpose make members of the Church of England what they are without the Sacraments in mature life, by what argument I should like to know can it be proved that it is not to their faith and integrity of purpose solely that members of the Roman Catholic Church are indebted likewise for all the progress they make ? The only test of the efficaciousness of the Sacraments appreciable by common sense lies in their influence upon conduct. If therefore it were capable of proof, as distinct from assertion, which it is not, both that all the Sacraments administered in the Church of England but one were shams : and all administered in the Church of Rome, without exception, realities,

how comes it that we are not incomparably more exalted charac-
ters ourselves than we were formerly : or that Roman Catholic
countries on the Continent are not incomparably more penetrated
to the core with Christianity than England ?   Both these points,
I dare say, might be affirmed by some : but they are denied, and I
maintain with much more reason, by others : and therefore at
best it can only be the degree to which the thing exists, not
whether it exists at all, which is in question.   I have already
spoken of the eloquent sermon I heard preached in Paris, in
which the Christian practices of my old friends in England were
held up for imitation.   The preacher himself had a history of
his own hardly less eloquent.   He had quitted the cure of one
of the most important churches in Paris to found a religious
community for the purpose of raising the tone of the French
clergy.   What had impelled him ?   Simply, the extremely
devout demeanour of two *ci-devant* Anglican clergymen lately
become Oratorians, whom he had watched saying their masses at
one of the altars in his own church from his confessional.   Certainly they could not have said a Roman Mass before they became
Roman Catholic priests ; but for all their preliminary training in
piety they were beholden as certainly to the Communion which
they had just quitted : so that they who had been educated in
Anglicanism were the means of suggesting to a Roman Catholic
priest in France how much room there was for improvement in
the training of his fellow clergy.   I have another anecdote to
tell of the same kind from what happened to me when in Spain
much more recently.   I spent the latter part of Lent, including
Holy Week, at Seville : and had looked forward to the ceremonies
immediately preceding Easter there with no small interest.   But
when the time for them arrived, I never saw services more
coldly conducted or more scantily attended, and ceremonies less
productive, in appearance at least, of any devotional feelings.   I
returned from them each time pained and scandalised.   About
the middle of Holy Week I fortunately had occasion to go to my
banker's ; and on entering I found a priest there waiting like

myself to be served. Something induced me to accost him in English, on his replying to me in the same, we soon entered warmly into conversation. He turned out to be a young priest who had " served his time " at the Brompton Oratory, though not a native of England. I confided to him what I thought of the services. He expressed no surprise: on the contrary he dissuaded my going again to the churches I named. " Come to our church," he said, " and I think you will see things done as they ought to be, and a very different style of congregation." I went and found it all as he had told me. There was life in the services, earnestness in the celebrants, devotion in the worshippers. The Brompton Oratory, that heart-stirring creation of old Oxford and Cambridge men, had sent out missionaries to evangelise Seville. Nobody who had frequented and compared it with the churches all round could dispute its claim to be the beginning of a new order of things there. As I am in Spain already, I may as well go on. From Seville I proceeded to a small village in the neighbourhood of the Sierra of most primitive description. There I remained several months. There was early Mass most mornings of the week : but I seldom, if ever, saw any but women at it : and these rarely more than from ten to twenty. But on Sundays at High Mass, the church, which was of considerable size for a village church, was crammed full of men and women, the former thronging the choir as far as it would contain them, where I sat myself. I took some pains to examine, but I never could discover anybody, man, woman, or child, in the whole congregation who used a book besides myself : and whatever may have been their inmost feelings, which I do not pretend to decipher, the countenances of the men bespoke nothing but listless apathy. Vespers were invariably attended by the priest, one cantor, and myself : in all, three, and to the best of my remembrance, never more. There were no evening services of any description while I was there. The only spark of devotion I ever witnessed—and I record it with as much pleasure—was that now and then I used to see parties of four or five women sitting outside their doors in the cool of the evening reciting their chaplet. The priest was affable and intelligent: and seemed anxious to promote education : but he was a good deal mixed up in the secular affairs of his neighbours as well : and the honours of his house were always done by one who went by the name of his "cugina," but I was laughed at for supposing it meant the relationship that we understand by it. I could only therefore account for the average respect that was paid him on the supposition that such things were not uncommon. Altogether I quitted this village feeling strongly that there was certainly not more real Christianity practised in it than in my own native parish in Wales, if so much : that the Welch there were better educated and more intelligent in their devotions beyond comparison than these specimens of Andalusia, and that the clergyman there could not at all events have a woman sitting at the head of his table who was neither his wife nor his relation. Yet this was a country that had remained exclusively Roman Catholic since its release from the Moors. From the south of Spain I proceed to the garden of France, the heart of Tourraine. There I passed some time pleasantly enough at a country house, long before I joined the Roman Catholic Church : yet I studied its workings then with no less interest. As there was no Anglican church within reach, I accompanied the family to the parish church, from two to three miles off, just about the distance of my own at home. Church-going was confined to Mass on Sundays, high or low: Low when any of the family communicated, which was never oftener than once a month ; High Mass otherwise. This was the only public service, to which anybody, speaking generally, went in the neighbourhood : and that over, everybody met, gossiped, and promenaded up and down the village till the carriages were ready to take them home. This was precisely the custom of my own neighbourhood : but with this difference, that most of the gentry came to church twice on Sundays, and some of them likewise to occasional services during the week in Lent, Advent, or Christmas-time. There was one circumstance connected with my Sundays in France, there or elsewhere, which I shall not easily forget. I was always asked to the best parties, and to the best hunting or shooting, on Sundays : and being a keen sportsman in those days, it was no small act of self-denial in obedience to my Anglican principles to forego the latter. Well ! the finest "battue" to which I ever had a chance of going was at an historic château not far from where I was staying in Tourraine, where, by the way, the church stood just outside the grounds, and the lady of the château, to her credit be it spoken, attended Mass daily : the usual congregation, however, being herself and the acolyte, besides the priest. As this battue was on Sunday, I declined it equally and went to church. Immediately before the Gospel—just in time to save Mass, that is —a bustle was heard outside the building which made the congregation look up : and presently the principal actors in the "chasse" entered, leaving their guns, dogs, and game with their retainers in the porch, who were thus corporally present. With the last Gospel they had disappeared to resume their sport. I thought then, and still think, that so far we did things in reality better in England a hundredfold, notwithstanding that appearances were kept up there. I could fill a volume with anecdotes to the same effect, all gathered from personal experience during my travels abroad in most parts of Europe and round the Mediterranean : but I can only find space here for one more, which I select from the point of comparison still being with my own native parish in Wales. This parish was a Vicarage from which the Incumbent drew £150 a year or thereabouts, and a dignitary of the Mother Church of the diocese £1100 or £1200 a year. The Ecclesiastical Commissioners have since removed this grievance—a practical grievance it was—and have subdivided the parish. Passing one summer at Porto di Fermo when it was Papal territory, I frequented the church there, which was always well attended by both sexes, on week-days as on Sundays, and was greatly edified by the earnestness and devotion of the parish priest. I inquired what his salary was, and was told, and if I remember right he confirmed it to me with his own lips, that it amounted to no more than £80 or two thousand francs. The Cardinal Archbishop, some of the parishioners told me with much warmth, was in the enjoyment of what we should call the great tithes: "and we never see him," they added, "except as he passes to or from his *villeggiatura* in the neigh-- bourhood where he spends his vast wealth." I cannot, of course, vouch for the entire accuracy of their statements, I only know that they described it as a gross abuse : and were them- selves amongst those most constant at church. Possibly this grievance may not exist now.

To come to my conclusions. The conviction impressed upon me by what I have heard and seen at home and abroad is that English Christianity—by which I mean that of members of the Church of England in general, I cannot speak from experience of any other—is as good and genuine, and for ordinary pur- poses as beneficial, as what is found in other nations—France, Spain, and Italy, for instance—so that either it is produced, fed, and nourished by all the Sacraments, as theirs is : or else, pro- duced, fed, and nourished by a single Sacrament, it penetrates society and forms character to the same extent as that which has the support of all the Sacraments, and is no less efficacious for good in most other respects. It may be isolated, but such is the position of England politically as well as geographically : its peculiarities are of a piece with the national character, itself having its weak as well as its strong side: its shortcomings, historically traceable to the sins of our forefathers in no small degree. Among the strong points attributable to its influences are a strong love of honesty in intention, of truthfulness in lan- guage, and of uprightness and manliness in conduct : and a still stronger abhorrence of falsehood and treachery to engagements in every form. Its virtues belong mostly to the practical and domestic order. Its weak points are too great self-reliance, too much disposition to criticise, too little faith in the Unseen. As

a general rule, Roman Catholics are weak where Anglicans are
strongest, and strong where Anglicans fail. Such results are due
to the system in each case, shewing imperfections in each.
Anglicans may be compared with Roman Catholics in this
country, as boys brought up at a public school in England with
boys brought up at a private school or else at home. Anglicans may
be compared with Roman Catholics abroad as men educated at
Oxford or Cambridge with men educated at the Universities of
Paris, Munich, or Padua. Fundamentally, their faith and practice is the same : but they have been formed after different models
in both. I trust the day is not far distant when the religiously
minded in both Communions will insist on associating together as
brethren, and learning from each other as Christians, and com-
bining for works of charity without distinction of nations. Too
long—much too long—have they been kept in ignorance of each
other, and thus prevented improving each other, through prejudice.
The two points on which alone I notice any sensible difference
between my own devotional practices in former days and now,
are praying for the souls of the departed and invoking the saints
in glory. Both practices I can unhesitatingly pronounce from
experience to be full of comfort and profit, of elevating and puri-
fying influences : I am sorry for those who live in ignorance or
neglect of them : and I can hardly imagine any person who has
tried them in a spirit of faith honestly abandoning them. Still
every fresh page I read of Church history in the 14th and 15th
centuries convinces me more and more of the awful profanity
that had attached to both in those days, and as even in the
Roman Catholic manuals of devotion I use myself there are frequent hyperboles of language that I could never adopt, and
should desire to see cancelled above all things,* I cannot consider

---

* I instance but one such, p. 29 of our *Vade Mecum*, "O holy Virgin Mary,
Mother of Mercy, *preserve me this night from all evil, whether of body or soul.*"
The meaning of course is, "Pray God to preserve me." How much more would
it have cost to have had this printed in full : or how much longer time would it
take to say? I must add that I constantly hear sermons [up and down England]
on S. Mary that are little more than legends, drawn from the Apocryphal
Gospels, or no better source.

the excessive caution of the Church of England altogether directed against a thing of the past, and without excuse now. Words employed in non-natural senses are dangerous stumbling-blocks in any Communion. Our own liturgical offices were carefully weeded at the time of the Council of Trent, and contain no such extravagances. It would be well if we were never on any pretext allowed to exceed their measured language in our private forms. Neither our liturgical forms, indeed, as they now exist, any more than our private forms, embodying such devotions, were known to the primitive Church : and therefore the lack of them in the Church of England, however much to be regretted on all accounts, cannot affect the essence, though it may impair the tenderness, of the Christianity taught and imbibed there. I am therefore satisfied that the Christianity taught and imbibed there differs in no fundamental quality from that with which I have been conversant since joining the Roman Communion. I am morally certain that I have frequented the same Sacraments in both with profit : consequently I feel that I could die equally well in the one or the other : and can see no reason for changing from one to the other except on *secondary* grounds, or unless driven to it. " When they persecute you in this city "—of *Israel*, that is— " flee ye into another " was not said for the Apostles alone. In conclusion, it is my firm persuasion still—indeed much more so than in 1853, when I published my first book *—that should Christendom ever be re-united, it will go down to posterity as having been brought about mainly by those who had been born and educated in the Church of England.

With these convictions, it may seem superfluous in me to add my belief that having been ordained priest in the Church of England, I am a priest still. But I desire to state this explicitly because of the disparagement lately cast upon Anglican Orders on general grounds by a great name amongst us. To the historical argument he will have nothing to say : therefore I will only remark on it, that having examined it thoroughly, I am as

* Called the " Counter-Theory," pp. 212—23.

convinced of its tenableness as of anything of the kind in Church history. And as to the form, on which he is equally reserved, I can only say that either the Anglican ordinals in use now or formerly must be allowed adequate, or else most of the primitive forms—to say nothing of those still used in the East—must be pronounced inadequate. On jurisdiction, I need not reiterate what I have said already, or am about to say. "Who is the *custos* of the Anglican Eucharist?" is his chief difficulty. "Could I, without distressing or offending an Anglican, describe what sort of *custodes* they—the Anglican clergy—have been and are to their Eucharist?" My Lord, it is anything but my intention to excuse or extenuate the scandalous irreverence that prevailed shortly before our own days, and I fear is not extinct yet, amongst Anglican clergymen in administering the Sacraments of the Church: but I cannot shut my eyes to the fact that it followed naturally from their low views of them, and that their low views of them were precipitated by the audacity that centuries ago was not afraid to say of the Eucharist, "Sacerdos creat Deum;" of penance, "Deus remittit culpam: Papa vero culpam et pœnam," and the like. But, taking our own views of the Blessed Eucharist into account, is there or has there been any tale of irreverence towards it amongst Anglicans, comparable for horrors with the history of poisoned chalices and poisoned Hosts amongst ourselves formerly, the extent of which is made patent to this day by the special precautions taken whenever the Pope celebrates Mass most solemnly, that no such harm may befal him—"Avant qu'il arrive"—I am quoting from a well-known précis of the ceremonies at Easter in Rome—"on a coutume de faire l'épreuve des espèces de la manière suivante : Le Diacre prend une des trois hosties qu'il a mises en ligne droit sur la patène, et la rend au Prélat-Sacriste. Quand celui-ci l'a reçu, le Cardinal-diacre prend de nouveau l'une des deux qui reste : et après l'avoir fait toucher intérieurement et extérieurement au calice et à la patène, il la consigne au Prélat-Sacriste, qui doit la consommer aussitôt, ainsi que la première, le visage tourné vers le Pape. Le troisième et dernière hostie est employée pour le sacrifice. Le Cardinal prend les burettes du vin et de l'eau, en vers' un peu dans la coupe, que lui présente le Prélat-Sacriste, dont ce dernier doit boire immédiatement le contenu."*

Such perversion of the life-giving Sacrament to destroy life, as had to be specially guarded against in this way whenever the Vicar of Christ pontificated, is absolutely without parallel in the annals of the Anglican Church since the Reformation. So that notwithstanding our high views of it, the worst known profanations of it have been amongst ourselves.

I admit that up to the time of my inquiring into the true causes of the earlier schism between the East and West, I was not prepared to look upon the position of the Church of England as favourably as I do now : because I regarded it as the effect of schism—wilful and deliberate schism—on her part in separating from the Communion to which she had been so long bound, and over which, with the full concurrence of her clergy and laity for ages, Rome ruled supreme. I expressed this unhesitatingly three years back in the first part of my book,† and am far from intending to retract *all* that I said then : but having since discovered the general system of Church government in which England, in common with all other Western nations, had up to that time acquiesced, to have been based upon forgeries, and opposed to the genuine code of the Church, I as unhesitatingly recognise the right—nay, the duty paramount—of every local Church to revolt against such a concatenation of spurious legislation as this, and scattering to the winds every link of the false chain that had enthralled it hitherto, to return to the letter and spirit of those genuine canons, stamped with the assent of the whole Church, and never repealed. Supposing this done, even the act of S. Augustine and his companions in establishing the jurisdiction of the patriarch of the West over this island is found illegal, having been declared null and void by anticipation in the eighth Canon of the Council of Ephesus already quoted : " So that none of the bishops most beloved by

* L'année Liturgique, p. 158.   † Christendom's Divisions, pp. 198—223.

God do assume any other province that is not, or was not formerly and from the beginning, subject to him, or those who were his predecessors. . . . But if any one introduce a regulation contrary to the present determination, the Holy General Synod decrees that it be of no force." It is idle, or worse than idle, to assert that S. Augustine found England subject to Rome when he arrived : and it is quite true that he accomplished its subjection two centuries and a half or more previously to the publication of the pseudo-decretals ; but it is no less true that its subjection was accomplished in the teeth of this canon, as well as of the protest* of the native episcopate that he found in possession. It may well be doubted whether S. Gregory was ever properly made acquainted with their prescriptive claims : in any case, what was then effected with his sanction was precisely what S. Leo the Great informed the East the canons would not allow of his con- ceding to the Constantinopolitan patriarch Anatolius at the fourth Council. The wily forger of the pseudo-decretals had his eye upon all such "accomplished facts" in the West when he compiled his code, and either founded his maxims upon them or else sought to legitimatise them by the high authority which he claimed for his maxims. Both, therefore, necessarily belong to the same category : neither can one possibly stand without the other. Anglican divines have long cited this ordinance of the Council of Ephesus in proof of their canonical independence of the jurisdiction of Rome : but they ought in fairness to have acknowledged themselves at the same time bound by the Sardican canons, that British bishops assisted in passing, admitting and regulating appeals to the Pope. This, I conceive, will be found to be the true limit of what is due to the Pope from England, according to the genuine law of the Church. The primatial See of England, whether at Caerleon or elsewhere, was originally independent and autocephalus, and never should have been made amenable to his jurisdiction as patriarch, whether for consecration or any similar purpose.

* Given in Cave, Church Govt., p. 251, from Spelman's Concil. Brit., A.D. 601.

I am well aware, my Lord, that this last inference of mine must cut at the very root of your position in England, should it prove correct: but as I have lived in the investigation of these questions for the last twenty years and upwards, you will scarce accuse me of being influenced by personal considerations in getting to their final solution. On the contrary, my wish is to give everybody the fullest credit for a sensitive conscience that I claim myself. Neither is it against individuals nor yet systems, but abuses and perversions of systems, that I wage war. When I was in the enjoyment of a Fellowship at Oxford we were all living in the hourly neglect of statutes which every one of us had sworn to observe, and I was one of those who demanded that either those statutes should be repealed formally, or else kept honestly. Still as our breaches of them had accumulated gradually, and become law insensibly, how could I have laid the blame of them on the existing or immediately preceding generations of Heads and Fellows, and reviled them as unprincipled or dishonest men? In the same way I mean neither disrespect nor disaffection to the living authorities of the Roman Catholic Church, when I draw attention to the undeniable fact that they are daily violating the law of the Church. What I criticise has been the work of centuries, commenced ages since, and what all of them together, were they ever so righteously minded, could not possibly change all at once, still less make perfection. Again, what I criticise is not the faith of the Popes, but their governmental policy, and that only since they became temporal princes as well as bishops, and not before. Their court and see having been all one for practical purposes since the establishment of the former, it would be vain to attempt drawing the line between them, especially as it is their joint action upon the Church, not upon empires or men in general, to which the verdict of history is most adverse. I am well aware, and have frequently spoken, of the services rendered by Rome to the nations of Europe, morally, socially, and religiously, in promoting their civilisation, in many respects a most up-hill task; and for these I am inclined to think there are some arrears of gratitude still due to it from Europe, and perhaps never likely to be settled, though I suppose none benefited more largely by their achievements in the middle ages than the Popes themselves. But when I contemplate the divisions of Christendom, past and present, and search history for their origin, I find it is the conduct of the Popes, more than anything else, for the last thousand years, in governing the Church, which has divided the Church. First of all, they allowed crowned heads to tamper with the Creed of the Church, if not to the unsettling of her faith, at least to the dividing of her household. Secondly, they allowed a spurious code to be brought into gradual use, without troubling themselves to refer to their own archives for proofs of its origin, and ultimately to overlay and be taken for the genuine laws of the Church. Thirdly, they countenanced one part of the Church, then in a minority, making war upon, and taking possession of, not merely the temporalities, but the ecclesiastical revenues and sees of the other part of the Church, then in a majority, to the ruin of Christianity, and triumphing of the Crescent over the Cross in those parts eventually, whence the Gospel had first sped. They countenanced all this, because it brought gain and aggrandisement to themselves and to their see, conformably with the maxims of the false, but in opposition to the maxims of the true code. Fourthly, as I have proved elsewhere,* they put off reforming the Church in their own patriarchate by fair means, till Providence permitted that it should be done by foul. Such is the verdict of history upon their conduct as Church governors since they became princes. I am far from pretending to have brought to light any facts that are not well known, though I may have grouped them together in one focus.

This being the case, my Lord, I ask how it is that there is not the slightest allusion to these facts in the invitations which have been issued to the forth-coming Council ? Rome has spoken : but I can discover nothing in what she has said like a confession

* Christendom's Divisions, Part I. pp. 128—153.

of sins, or of the justice of God in punishing them—expressions
of regret for the past, or promises of amendment in future.
All Christendom has gone astray save she.   Of all institutions,
the Popedom alone stands erect : has never erred on any subject
whatever, has never been otherwise than what it is now : has
preserved its integrity, as well as its faith, unsullied.   It alone
has never caused divisions, or driven Christians into revolt : it
alone has never done anything for which it has cause to blush or
repent.   " I am and none else beside me . . . I shall be as a lady
for ever : I shall not sit as a widow, neither shall I know the loss
of children."—Babylon loquitur, non Jerusalem.   Three hundred
years ago there was a Pope who spoke differently, and told men
the truth.   With what general applause, and sympathy of the
good and earnest in all lands, would such candour as his have
been reciprocated, had it been copied in what we have just heard !
" You will also say," continued Adrian VI. to his legate, " that
we frankly admit that God has permitted this judgment to fall
upon His Church for the sins of men, chiefly priests and prelates
of the Church . . . We know that in this holy seat there have
been many enormities, now for some years past, and abuses in
spiritual things, excesses in what has been ordained, all things
in short perverted . . . Wherefore, it is necessary that we should
all give glory to God, and humble our souls before Him, and see
each one of us from whence he hath fallen."

An invitation to a general humiliation might well have preceded
invitations from the Pope to any Council for re-uniting Christendom.   Again, in inviting people to a Council for that purpose,
was it wise to insult them ?   The Easterns are adjured to come
to it as their predecessors came to the Councils of Lyons and
Florence : but to each of these Councils the authorities of the
Eastern Church received a formal invitation, designating them
by their respective titles, and at the Council of Florence sat
and deliberated with Western bishops upon equal terms : nor was
it till they were gone, that deputies from the descendants of
heretical bodies—Nestorian or Monophysite—were introduced.

All bishops of the Eastern rite, no matter what their antecedents, are placed in the same category by Pius IX.: for what purpose, unless to deter the most considerable from coming, it would be difficult to say. In the same way, non-Catholics, that is to say, non-Roman Catholics, are treated as a rabble without guides, a flock without shepherds, indiscriminately: as though all had been equally bereft of organisation, and all alike were devoid of intelligence. Yet part of this rabble has lived under episcopal government for 300 years, and every endeavour was made to get bishops sent from it to the Council of Trent, and it knows something of the controversy between it and Rome, to say the least. Then what of its mighty offshoots in the New World and in the Colonies? Altogether the latent "animus" that unprejudiced persons would be likely to detect in both invitations is, that they should be declined—declined in order that, the Council being confined to those beholden to the Pope for their mitres, his prerogatives might be secured against losing, even if they should not gain, anything by its meeting.

If it is otherwise—if Rome is sincerely bent upon re-uniting Christendom—the whole thing lies in a nutshell, and is in fact already done. Two maxims honestly carried out would alone suffice for re-uniting Christendom. The first is ancient and well known: "Nullum tempus præscribit Ecclesiæ." This is apt in general to be applied to Church lands and endowments. It must apply with infinitely more force to Church laws, accepted everywhere, that have never been repealed. No mere disuetude can make them null and void. The other maxim has recently been chosen in this controversy for their motto by a learned body, to whom I am never tired of confessing my obligations, the Society of Jesus in England—"Peace through the truth." If they will only bring their immense influence to bear in enforcing this maxim wherever falsehood is proved, one of the first consequences will be that the False Decretals, and all that has been founded on them, will go to the wall. I have already quoted the opinion of their learned brethren on the other side of

the water, to the effect that this spurious code supplanted the
discipline that had reigned paramount in the Church up to that
time, and is the basis of the discipline that reigns now. Let it be
repudiated honestly, therefore, and the ancient discipline of the
Church will once more be revived in full force. Let us see what
effect this would have on the divisions of Christendom. First,
in accordance with the dogmatic canon appended to the definition
of the 4th, 5th, and 6th Councils, the Nicene Creed would cease
to be used in any but the form in which it existed then. I need
hardly remind your Lordship that as it existed then, the article
in dispute was couched in Christ's own words : " Who proceedeth
from the Father "—His words that we have presumed to improve
upon in the form we use—By returning to them, we should,
in reality, be but deferring to Him. This, alone, would do
away with the principal ground of strife between the East and
West. Secondly, Rome would be confined, for ordinary jurisdiction, to the original bounds of her patriarchate according to
the 8th canon of the Council of Ephesus, in other words, to the
Continent of Europe : but she would receive appeals from
England and the rest of the West according to the Sardican
canons. Appeals from the East would be carried to Constantinople, in conformity with the 9th and 17th canons of the Council
of Chalcedon. Thus the principal ground of strife between
England and Rome would be removed on the one hand, and all
intermeddling by Rome with the affairs of the East on the other.
Latin patriarchs of Greek sees would be out of the question.
A General Council, with the Pope in the first, and the Patriarch
of Constantinople in the second place, would be the last
resort—as the African bishops told Pope Celestine was the
true purport of the Nicene canons—for all alike. Thirdly,
what is of infinitely more importance to Christians generally,
desirous of living in peace and charity with their brethren
all the world over, no profession of faith would be required
from any seeking to be admitted to Communion in any Church,
but the Nicene Creed, according to the solemn import of the

canon with which we commenced. When it was passed, all the modern controversies on grace had been anticipated by the followers of Pelagius, and there had been questions raised about the sacraments and rites of the Church similar to those amongst which we live. And still the language of that canon is most emphatic—"Those coming over *from whatsoever heresy* to the communion of the Church, are to be made to subscribe to the Nicene Creed and no other." The Creed of Pius IV. might be retained as discipline for the clergy, but it could no longer be imposed on the laity. Plain Christians might therefore traverse the world with no other passport to the Sacraments of the Church in all lands than the Nicene Creed.

Christendom is one before God, and *de jure*, so long as these laws form part of the code of the Church, and are not repealed. It is only disunited *de facto*, because they are infringed, and the executive of the Church is indifferent, or else a party, to their infringement. If Rome is really the executive of the Church, as she claims to be, is really desirous of unity, she has nothing to do but bestir herself to bring herself and all others to observe the laws. I have heard some persons assert positively that she will never be capable of this effort till she has been both disestablished and disendowed. May they be false prophets !

I have the honour to be,

My Lord Archbishop,

Your obedient and obliged servant,

E. S. Ff.

Octave of S. Edmund, 1868.

London : Swift & Co., Regent Press, 55, King Street, Regent Street, W.

www.ingramcontent.com/pod-product-compliance
Lightning Source LLC
Chambersburg PA
CBHW021514090426
42739CB00007B/603